EASY
Arts & Crafts
FOR KIDS

Pantyhose Silk Screen, *page 56*

EASY
Arts & Crafts
FOR KIDS

50 Fun Projects
TO MAKE, WEAR, AND SHARE

JENNIFER PERKINS

ROCKRIDGE
PRESS

For general information on our other products and services or to obtain technical support, please contact our Customer Care Department within the United States at (866) 744-2665, or outside the United States at (510) 253-0500.

Rockridge Press publishes its books in a variety of electronic and print formats. Some content that appears in print may not be available in electronic books, and vice versa.

Interior & Cover Designer: Jay Dea
Art Producer: Janice Ackerman
Editors: Jeanine Le Ny and Eliza Kirby
Production Editor: Matthew Burnett

Front & Back Cover Photography: © 2019 Evi Abeler
Interior Photography: © 2019 Jennifer M. Ramos
Author Photo: © 2019 Jennifer M. Ramos

ISBN: Print 978-1-64152-713-2
eBook 978-1-64152-714-9
R0

This book is for Ding
and Dong, a.k.a. my creative
littles, who are constantly inspir-
ing and impressing me. Shout out to my
husband, who had no idea what he was getting
into when he married me. (Sorry about the glitter
everywhere, sweetie.) This book is also for my
dad, who taught me the meaning of hard
work, and my mom, who is the wind
beneath my crafty wings.

CONTENTS

INTRODUCTION IX

◆ ART START...1

Modern Art on Wood 2

Shaving Cream Marbling 4

Irresistible Watercolor Resist Art 7

No-Kill Cardboard Cactus 9

Way Out Weaving 12

Rolling-Pin Printing 16

Yarn Painting 18

Rooty Tooty Fruity Foil Art 20

◆ TOP-NOTCH TOYS...23

Spoon Puppets 24

Tin Can Robots 28

Fluffy and Fun Chalkboard Slime 31

Glow-in-the-Dark Chalk 34

Giant Bubble Wand 36

Mindful Jars 39

Painted Rock People 41

◆ CRAFTY FASHION...45

Super Cool Ice Dyeing 46

No-Sew Scrunchies 49

Paper Clip and Washi Tape Jewelry 52

Faux Sashiko Denim Patches 54

Pantyhose Silk Screen 56

Taco Sunglass Case 60

Tie-Dye Shoes 63

Shrink Plastic Flair 65

Tassel Key Chains 68

Sticker Resist T-Shirt 71

◆ GIFT IDEAS...75

Soap Pops 76

T-Shirt Notebook 79

Stitched Greeting
Cards 83

Best Friend Doughnut
Charm Necklaces 86

Rainbow Bath Bombs 90

◆ DIY DÉCOR IDEAS...95

Drip Pots 96

No-Sew Felt Pillow 99

Embroidery Hoop Wall
Pocket 103

Easy Woven Wall
Hanging 106

No-Sew Felt Enamel
Pin Banner 109

Cookie Cutter Ring
Dishes 111

Melty Bead Picture
Frame 114

Wrapped Desk Caddy 118

Paper Bag Hanging
Stars 121

Groovy Gravel Trays 124

Petite Pom-Pom Rug 126

◆ CRAFTING WITH NATURE AND CRAFTY UPCYCLES...131

Recycled Wrapped
Vase 132

Felted Wool Acorns 136

Sun Printing 139

Seed Balls 141

Pressed Leaf
Lanterns 144

Rolled Magazine
Storage 148

Recycled Hanging
Bottle Planter 151

Too Cute Trinket Jars 155

Custom String Lights 157

GLOSSARY...162 | RESOURCES...163 | INDEX...164

Recycled Hanging Bottle Planter, *page 151*

INTRODUCTION

Who here likes arts and crafts? Go ahead and shout it out even though I can't hear you (because you know a book has no ears). Now that I know you're on board, let's get down to crafty business!

This book has some seriously cool projects. We're talking things you are going to want to wear, give to your friends, and hang on your wall with pride. Get ready to be complimented by everyone you know on your creative handiwork. Plus, did I mention that they're all quick and easy? There is something for everyone!

Parents, if you are reading this, let me introduce myself: My name is Jennifer Perkins. I've been the editor-in-chief of a children's craft magazine and made oodles of kids' projects for places like HGTV and the DIY Network. I've also been a scout leader, taught kids' art classes, and have two littles of my very own. I know the importance of keeping crafts simple yet stylish—in other words, making projects that can be finished in one sitting with minimal supplies and still look like something you actually want to put up in your living room. Don't worry, parents: I've got your back! Most of these projects are things you are probably going to want to make yourself as well.

GETTING STARTED

You know how most books have you start at the beginning? Well, not this book, party people! Take a seat and flip through the pages. Let a project call to you. Does your wardrobe need some spicing up? Head over to the Crafty Fashion chapter (page 45). Is your room looking a bit drab? Check out the DIY Décor chapter (page 95). Dive right in, pick a project, and get started!

The most important thing to remember when getting artsy craftsy is that *you do you*. Just because a T-shirt in this book is shown in blue, red, and yellow does not mean you can't make your own purple, pink, and orange version. If you think sun printing with flowers instead of leaves would be better, go for it. Mix things up! This book is intended to inspire you. You will have all the instructions you need to complete the fun and easy projects in this book from start to finish, but always remember it does not have to look exactly like the pictures you see here. Put your own unique stamp on these ideas. Combine a couple of ideas, tweak a recipe, switch up the medium, or use a marker instead of paint. There is no right or wrong way to be creative.

Essential Tools and Materials

Each of these projects uses specific supplies, but there are a few staples every aspiring artist or crafter should have in their creative toolbox:

Craft Paint – Nontoxic craft paint usually costs less than a buck a color. One week's allowance could buy you an entire rainbow.

Paintbrushes – You can't paint a rainbow without a few of these. Every crafter and artist needs brushes, and you can buy a variety pack with different sizes. A personal favorite of mine is a round sponge-dauber brush for making the perfect polka dot. If you don't have one, the eraser on a pencil works great, too.

Yarn – Yarn is good for so much more than knitting and crochet. You could use it to hang your new recycled-bottle planter. Make a bouquet of pom-poms to put in a vase in your room. Whip up a chunky, funky tassel for your backpack. There are lots of uses for a single skein (that's a fancy term for a bunch of yarn).

Hot Glue Gun and Glue Sticks – Best used with the help of a parent, the hot glue gun is great when you need a strong adhesive that dries quickly.

A low-temperature hot glue gun doesn't get the glue quite as hot, which can be helpful for your project if you want to avoid too much heat.

Craft Glue – Not quite old enough to use the hot glue gun alone? No worries, a good thick nontoxic craft glue is your new best friend. You might have to wait a bit longer for things to dry, but remember that saying, "good things come to those who . . ."

Decoupage Medium – Is it a glue, is it a shiny, protective top coat, is it magic? It's all of those things and more. Just do yourself a favor and get a bottle, and you can thank me later.

Cardboard Box – Cardboard is good for so many things! You can transform it into a loom with a bit of twine. No canvas? No problem, when you have a piece of cardboard. Need some extra storage? You can wrap a cardboard box with cording or pieces of rolled magazine pages. If nothing else, it can hold all your craft supplies when you want to stay organized.

Safety Tips

There are a few safety measures to keep in mind with this book. Irons, ovens, and hot glue guns are hot enough to cause burns. You should always ask a parent or an adult to help you. Always make sure your paints, glues, and decoupage mediums are nontoxic and kid-safe. Look for the ⚠ for projects that will need extra adult supervision. Most of these projects are just fine for you to make on your own, but when in doubt, ask a grown-up. That's what they're there for. Finally, remember that if you use any tools out of the kitchen for crafting—cookie cutters, cookie sheets, cutting boards, or rolling pins—those tools can no longer be used on food. Be sure to keep your craft tools separate so there's no confusion.

A Crafter's Tips and Tricks

1

Treat your supplies with respect. Clean your brushes and put the lids back on your paint. Nothing worse than feeling creative only to realize your brush is rock-hard from last week's project.

2

Traditional craft supplies don't always need to be used traditionally. In this book, embroidery hoops become wall pockets and silk-screening machines.

3

Always think beyond the paintbrush. Get ready to paint and print with ice, shaving cream, and rolling pins.

6

Start to look at everything with crafty eyes. Could that old T-shirt with a stain get an ice dye makeover? Turn that canvas tote bag inside out and redesign the inside.

7

Save those plastic containers and reuse them to rinse your paintbrushes.

These are 10 pearls of quick, crafty wisdom to guide you on your creative journey:

4

Practice makes perfect; the more you create, the more creative you will become. You were not great at soccer the first time you kicked a ball.

5

Don't underestimate things you already have around the house. There is no need to go buy a brand-new canvas when you can always recycle an old one or use a piece of cardboard instead.

8

Take a walk outside and let nature inspire you. We use leaves, seeds, and the sun for a few of these projects. Remember artists were inspired long before the internet was invented.

9

Poster board is your new best friend. I always keep a sheet underneath my craft projects for easy cleanup.

10

Add a container of disposable cleaning wipes to your supply list to make cleanup quick and easy.

No-Kill Cardboard Cactus, *page 9*

ART START

They don't call it "*arts* and crafts" for nothing. In this chapter we'll create lots of art pieces while practicing some basic crafting techniques, such as repeating patterns, marbling, and working with a resist. We will also learn unconventional tricks for making cool stuff with yarn, rolling pins, aluminum foil, and food coloring. With the techniques in this chapter you will have the basics for all kinds of artsy craftsy fun. Art comes in all different shapes, sizes, and colors—not just paint on a canvas (though I love that method too). Let's spill some paint on purpose, bust out the shaving cream, and have some fun!

Modern Art on Wood

This project is a spin on the clean lines of modern art. The secret is using masking tape to get those lines perfectly straight. This technique can be used on paper, fabric, or in this case, a wood panel. There is no right or wrong way to create your pattern; just like with a modern painter, art is in the eye of the beholder.

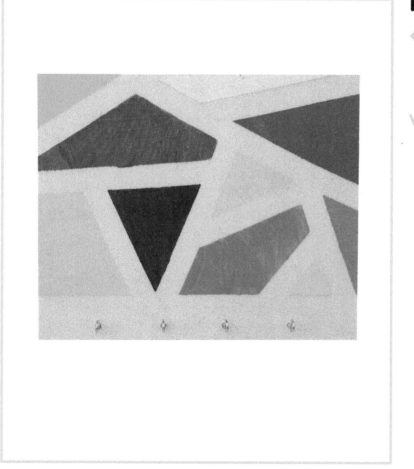

MESSY METER

1 2 3 4 5

WHAT YOU NEED:

- Wood panel (size depends on how large you want your art piece)
- Masking tape
- Craft paint (as many colors as you would like)
- Paintbrush
- Decoupage medium
- Sponge brush

WHAT YOU DO:

1. Tape off a random abstract pattern onto the wood using masking tape. Feel free to overlap pieces. Make sure that the tape is pressed down well.

2. Paint the shapes inside of the taped areas with different colors.

3. Allow the paint to dry completely and then remove the tape. Apply 1 to 2 coats of a shiny top coat, like a decoupage medium, using a sponge brush.

Shaving Cream Marbling

Have you ever used shaving cream to marble paint? Once you learn the fundamentals of marbling, this technique has all kinds of applications: modern art, custom stationery, textile design, and more. Food coloring from the kitchen pantry acts as your paint in this process.

WHAT YOU NEED:

- Disposable tray (such as an aluminum foil pan)
- Foam-based shaving cream
- Smoothing tool (paint spatula, ruler, or school ID)
- Food coloring (in as many colors as you would like to use)
- Toothpick
- Cardstock

1. Fill a disposable tray with shaving cream. Smooth the shaving cream flat with the smoothing tool.

2. Squirt drops of food coloring in a random pattern. Drag a toothpick lightly across the surface.

3. Drag a toothpick across the surface going in the other direction.

4. Lay the cardstock on the shaving cream. Gently push down on the paper until the cream starts coming up on the sides.

Continued →

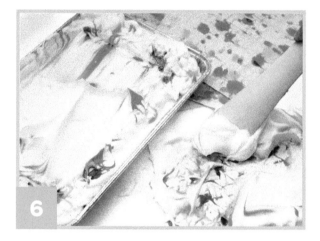

5. Remove the paper from the shaving cream and place it on a flat surface.

6. In one continuous motion, scrape the shaving cream down the paper using the smoothing tool. This creates the marbled effect.

7. Allow the shaving cream to dry. You can make paper beads, custom stationery, or abstract art to hang.

Irresistible Watercolor Resist Art

Fun fact: Wax repels water. Use this concept with crayons to create some unique art. You can draw a design freehand or, in this case, use a stencil.

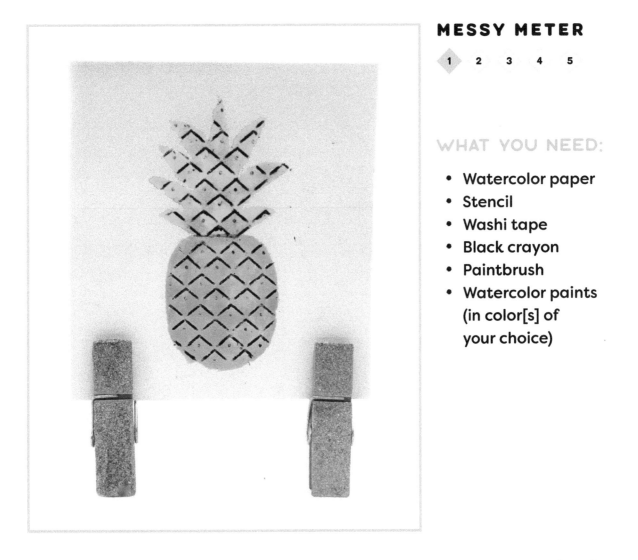

MESSY METER

1 2 3 4 5

WHAT YOU NEED:

- Watercolor paper
- Stencil
- Washi tape
- Black crayon
- Paintbrush
- Watercolor paints (in color[s] of your choice)

Continued →

WHAT YOU DO:

1. Tape the stencil to the watercolor paper so that it does not move.

2. Color in the stencil with the black crayon. Be careful not to move the stencil and to completely fill in the image. Everywhere there is crayon, the paint will not show. Remove the stencil.

3. Paint the entire sheet of paper with watercolor. This can be rainbows, an ombré pattern, or a solid color. The paint will color all of the areas not protected by the black crayon.

4. Allow the paint to dry and hang the picture.

No-Kill Cardboard Cactus

Finally, a plant you can't kill no matter how black your thumb is! No light or water is necessary for this pretty plant: just paint, cardboard, and toothpicks. Think of it as plant art.

MESSY METER

1 2 3 4 5

WHAT YOU NEED:

- Cardboard
- Pen
- Scissors
- Green paint
- Green paint pen (in a lighter shade than the green paint)
- Toothpicks
- Craft glue
- Vase or planter

Continued →

No-Kill Cardboard Cactus, continued

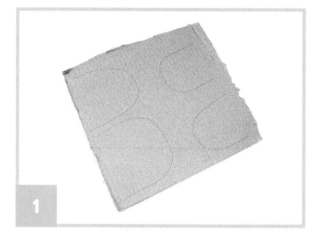

1. Trace out the shape of 4 cactus paddles onto a piece of cardboard.

2. Cut out all the shapes. The cactus can be as big or small as you like.

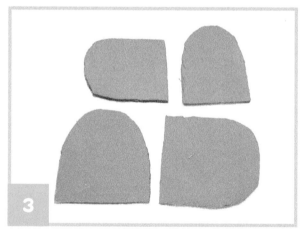

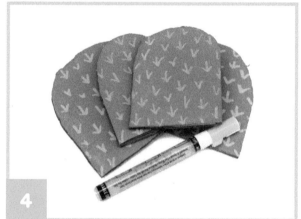

3. Paint all the paddles green on the front and let dry completely. Flip the paddles over and paint the backs green, too. Let dry completely.

4. Draw cactus spines on the paddles with the paint pen. These can be V shapes or arrows. Let dry completely.

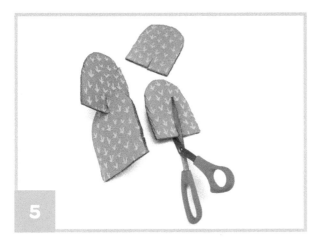

5. Cut 3-inch long slits into the paddles so that the cactus will fit together like a puzzle.

6. Break off the tips of toothpicks and attach to the sides of the cactus with craft glue. One toothpick every inch or so.

7. Put the cactus in a vase, planter, or jar. Sit back and admire your new work of (vegetative) art.

Way Out Weaving

Weaving is a trendy craft that is a lot easier than it looks, and all you need are a cardboard box and some yarn. With weaving, the important thing to remember is that there are two main parts: the warp and the weft. The warp is the twine you will use to create the cardboard loom. The weft is the yarn you will be weaving with.

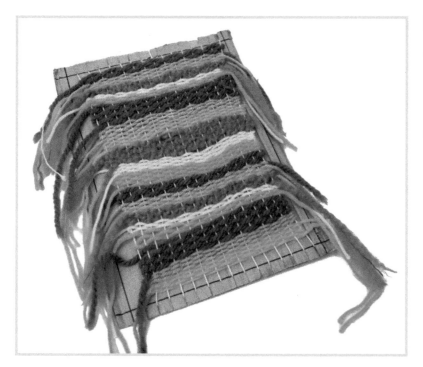

MESSY METER

1 2 3 4 5

WHAT YOU NEED:

- Cardboard Box
- Scissors
- Ruler
- Pen
- Twine
- Tape
- Yarn

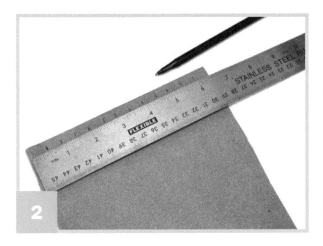

1. Cut a piece of cardboard the size you would like for your weaving to be. The size of a sheet of printer paper, or 8½ × 11 inches, is a good starting size.

2. Using a ruler, measure and mark every half inch along the top and the bottom of the cardboard. This spacing can be adjusted according to your preference and skill level. The wider apart the marks, the less weaving that will need to be done. The closer together the marks, the tighter the weave.

3. Cut a ½-inch slit into each mark along the top and the bottom of the cardboard.

Continued →

4. Start with a long tail of twine in the back and weave the twine up and down into the slits of the cardboard loom. This will create your warp, which will be what you weave on.

5. Tape the extra twine to the back of the loom when you are finished. Now you are ready to start weaving.

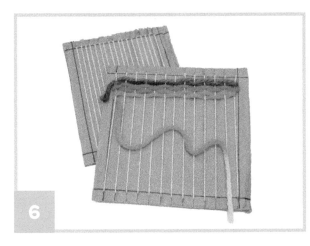

6. Starting at the top left, insert your yarn underneath the first string in your warp. Then weave it over and under the warp and repeat until you reach the end. Turn and weave over and under in the other direction. You can use one color or change out the yarn colors as you go.

7. When changing colors, if the yarn runs out in the middle of the loom, you can always attach another piece by tying the two together in a knot. Trim off the excess and continue as you were before.

8. Once you have covered the entire loom, there are two options. First, you can trim the raw edges and tuck them under the weaving. If you decide to trim the edges, leave at least 1 inch of yarn to prevent unraveling and so that you have something to tuck. The second option is to leave the edges hanging long for a more organic, boho look.

Rolling-Pin Printing

We're making art, not baking! This unique way of creating a repeat pattern is great for textiles, paper, and more. We're using ready-made stickers for this project, but you can always create your own designs with sticky-back craft foam. Remember that once you use the rolling pin with paint, it can no longer be used for baking.

MESSY METER

WHAT YOU NEED:

- Rolling pin
- Foam stickers
- Craft paint
- Aluminum foil (at least the width of the rolling pin)
- Scrap fabric or paper

1

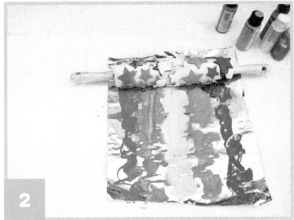

2

1. Apply stickers to the rolling pin in a random pattern. Remember to use foam stickers, as they are raised. It is also important that all the stickers be the same thickness.

2. Add craft paint to foil. Roll the pin through the paint, making sure all the stickers are covered in paint.

3. Place the paper or fabric on a flat surface. In one movement, roll the pin across the fabric. Repeat until entire surface is covered.

4. Once the paint has dried, hang your creation.

Yarn Painting

Try something different and "paint" your next project with yarn. The key is to keep your design simple and bold. Draw your own freehand image or trace a simple picture from a coloring book or printed off the internet. Yarn comes in so many colors and textures, and the possibilities of what you can create are endless.

MESSY METER

1 2 3 4 5

WHAT YOU NEED:

- Canvas or piece of wood
- Pencil
- Thick craft glue
- Small paintbrush
- Yarn
- Scissors

1. Draw or trace a design onto a canvas or flat piece of wood.

2. Working one section at a time, fill in the image with thick craft glue. You may need to use a small paintbrush to get all the edges. Using a piece of yarn about the length of your fingertip to your elbow apply the yarn to the wet glue. Trim and add more as needed.

3. Continue until the entire surface is covered. Feel free to paint unfinished edges with craft paint.

Rooty Tooty Fruity Foil Art ◆

When permanent markers meet foil, something special happens: extra shiny art. Freehand designs with pen and foil are fun, but raising the image with a glue outline gives it depth. This technique looks amazing on canvas as well as other flat surfaces like raw wood boxes or frames from the craft store. Remember to ask for help from an adult when working with hot glue, even a low-temperature glue gun.

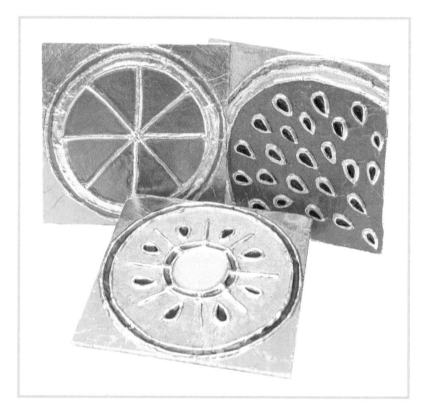

MESSY METER

1 2 3 4 5

WHAT YOU NEED:

- Canvas
- Pen
- Thick craft glue or low-temp hot glue gun
- Aluminum foil
- Pencil
- Permanent markers

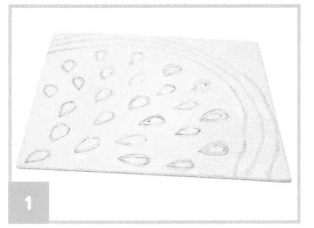

1

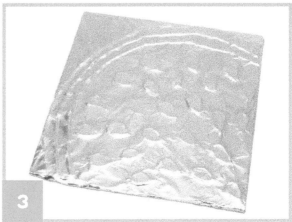

3

1. Draw an image onto your canvas. Simple designs will work best.

2. Apply thick craft glue or hot glue directly over the lines of the drawing. Allow glue to dry or cool completely.

3. Cover the entire canvas in foil with the shiny side facing out. Smooth the foil around the edges of the design using a pencil eraser or your fingertips. Don't press too hard or you might rip the foil. If you do make a small rip don't worry, just gently continue a few centimeters away.

4. Color the design with permanent markers. Leave the raised areas (where the glue is underneath) silver for an extra bit of pop.

Spoon Puppets, *page 24*

TOP-NOTCH TOYS

Craft up an afternoon of fun with these easy projects made from items you likely already have around the house. Rocks from the yard become interchangeable dolls or your own monster sets. Did you know you can make your own chalk in almost any color you want, and better yet you can make it glow-in-the-dark? Don't throw away those old tin cans, because you're going to make yourself a new robotic best friend.

Spoon Puppets

Always dreamed of seeing yourself on the big screen as an actor or actress? Start by getting plenty of practice with these spoon puppets. Wooden spoons make the perfect puppet canvas. You can embellish them with yarn hair and googly eyes or decorate them entirely with paint. The characters can be as wild and crazy as you want them to be. Don't forget to make a cereal-box puppet theater, too!

MESSY METER

1 2 3 4 5

WHAT YOU NEED:

- Wooden spoons
- Craft paint
- Paintbrush
- Craft glue
- Yarn
- Permanent markers
- Googly eyes
- Small bows, pipe cleaners, and trimming

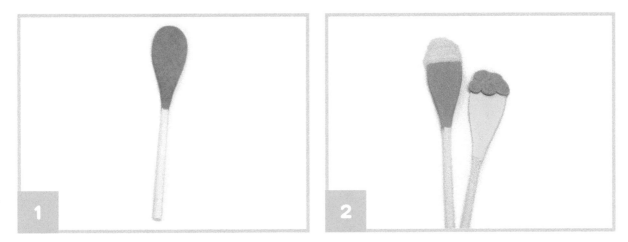

1. Paint the bowl part of each wooden spoon. These will be the puppets' faces. Allow the spoons to dry completely.

2. Add hair to the tops of the spoons using yarn and craft glue. You can try making updos with pom-poms, bangs with chunky yarn, or adding a bow as an accessory.

Continued →

Spoon Puppets, continued

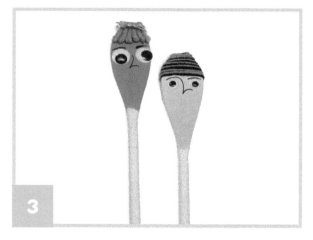

3

4

3. Draw facial features like eyebrows and noses with permanent markers, then glue on the googly eyes.

4. Glue on pipe cleaners, felt, yarn, or small bows to embellish the handles of the wooden spoons.

5

5. Prepare your stage for a dramatic reenactment of "Mystery in the 4th-Grade Lunch Room."

CEREAL-BOX PUPPET THEATER

Grab an empty cereal box and let's get those spoons ready for the spotlight!

WHAT YOU NEED:

- Cereal box
- Scissors
- Pen
- Paint
- Paintbrush
- Pom-pom fringe
- Glue

WHAT YOU DO:

1. Cut the cereal box open with a slit down the back. Remove tops and bottoms of box. Trace a square in the center.

2. Cut out the square shape. Paint the box and allow it to dry. Glue the pom-pom fringe along the inside top of the square opening. Once the glue has dried, refold along the fold lines to shape the box into the theater.

Tin Can Robots

Raid the kitchen and the tool box to make a batch of interchangeable robots. Nuts, bottle caps, and washers glued to small magnets make the perfect facial features. Use different-sized tin cans to make an entire family.

MESSY METER

WHAT YOU NEED:

- Tin cans
- Craft glue
- Small magnets
- Metal washers and nuts in various sizes
- Bottle caps
- Metal dish scrubbers
- Googly eyes

WHAT YOU DO:

1. Remove paper labels from tin cans. When working with empty cans, make sure they have been washed and rinsed and that the edges are smooth.

2. Glue washers and googly eyes into the underside of bottle caps to create facial features for your robots. Allow the glue to dry.

3. Glue small magnets on the other side of the bottle-cap facial features you created. Allow the glue to dry.

Continued →

Tin Can Robots, continued

4. Once the glue has dried, you can decorate your tin can robots. Mix and match facial features to create unique characters. The beauty of the magnets is that you can change your robots' faces again and again.

5. Metal scrubbers and steel wool can be glued on top of the can as hair for extra fun!

Fluffy and Fun Chalkboard Slime

Making and playing with slime never gets old with so many recipes available—colored, scented, fluffy, or crunchy, the slime options never end. Have you tried making chalkboard slime yet? Two-for-one: Draw some chalk marker pictures, then play with your slime, and repeat!

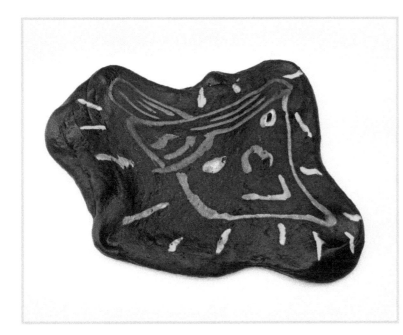

MESSY METER

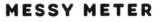

1 2 3 4 5

WHAT YOU NEED:

- Mixing bowl
- 1 cup glue
- ½ cup liquid starch
- 1 tbsp chalkboard paint
- Spoon
- ½ bag of Crayola Model Magic® clay
- Chalk markers

Continued →

Fluffy and Fun Chalkboard Slime, continued

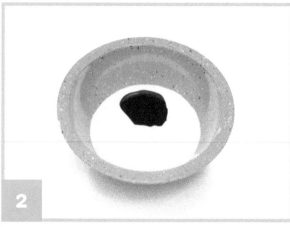

1. Measure out the glue, liquid starch, and chalkboard paint.

2. Combine ingredients in a mixing bowl.

3. Mix the 3 ingredients well until the slime starts to thicken. If the slime is still a little runny, add a bit more liquid starch a small amount at a time until the slime sets.

4. Once all of the ingredients are mixed well and no liquid starch remains in the bowl, add half a bag of clay; this is what makes the slime extra fluffy.

5. Use your hands to knead the clay and slime together.

6. Once everything is combined, you can use chalkboard markers to draw designs or write messages on the chalkboard slime.

7. In order to "erase" your chalkboard, just play with the slime as you usually would. The slime will absorb the chalk markers and you can start again.

Glow-in-the-Dark Chalk

Chalk is fun, but glow-in-the-dark chalk is even better! You can make your own chalk using a few simple ingredients. This batch glows, but you can tweak the recipe to make chalk with glitter or to change the color to anything you want. Silicone molds come in so many sizes and shapes that there's no need to make traditional sticks if you don't want to. Have fun with chalk shapes.

MESSY METER

1 2 3 4 5

WHAT YOU NEED:

- ½ cup plaster of paris (yields one color of chalk)
- 1 tsp glow-in-the-dark paint
- 1 tsp neon craft paint
- Warm water
- Disposable cups (one for each color of chalk)
- Wooden craft sticks (one for each color of chalk)
- Silicone mold

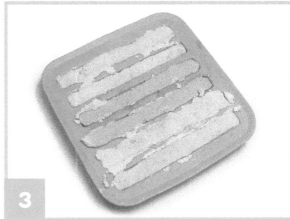

1. Each color of chalk will need its own disposable cup and wooden stick for stirring. Add ½ cup of plaster of paris to each cup.

2. Add 1 teaspoon of glow-in-the-dark paint and 1 teaspoon of neon paint to each cup. Stir with wooden craft sticks. If the plaster is still very thick, add warm water 1 teaspoon at a time until you get a runnier consistency.

3. Fill each mold with plaster mixture. Dry for 24 hours.

4. Remove chalk from the molds. If the plaster still feels wet to the touch, allow the chalk to dry for another 24 hours.

5. Use your new glow-in-the-dark chalk on chalkboards and sidewalks.

Giant Bubble Wand ◆

The only things better than bubbles are *really* BIG bubbles. In this project you will make your own giant bubble wand and learn the secret to making the biggest bubbles ever.

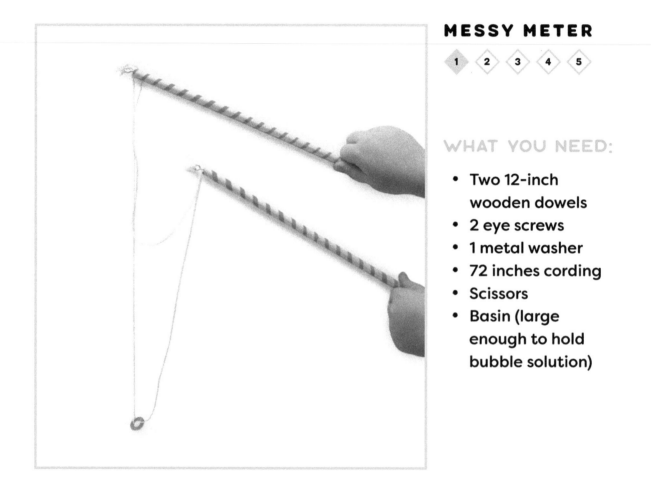

WHAT YOU NEED:

- Two 12-inch wooden dowels
- 2 eye screws
- 1 metal washer
- 72 inches cording
- Scissors
- Basin (large enough to hold bubble solution)

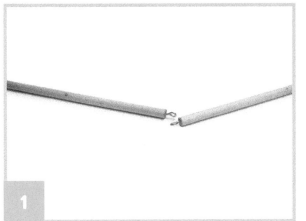

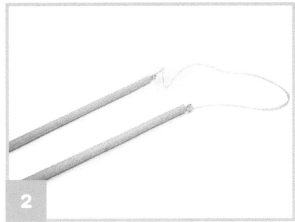

1. Twist a small eye screw into the end of each dowel. It can be screwed in by hand, but you may need a parent's help for this step.

2. Cut a piece of cording that is 24 inches long. Tie each end of the cording through an eye screw on the tip of each dowel.

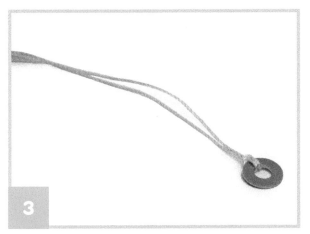

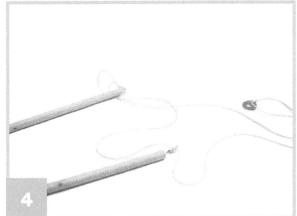

3. Cut a second piece of cording that is 48 inches long. Attach a washer to the center of the string.

4. Tie each end of the longer piece of cording to the eye screws as well.

Continued →

Giant Bubble Wand, continued

5. Dip the giant wand into the bubble solution and gently pull upwards. Swing the dowels around to allow air to travel through the cording and form a giant bubble.

GIANT-BUBBLE SOLUTION

WHAT YOU NEED:

- Basin
- 6 cups distilled water
- ½ cup dishwashing liquid (plain is best, not ultra or antibacterial)
- 2 tbsp glycerin

WHAT YOU DO:

Pour all the ingredients into the basin and let sit for at least an hour or more. You'll then be ready to make jumbo bubbles.

Mindful Jars ◈

Everybody needs the occasional reminder to be more mindful and in the moment. This just got much easier with your new DIY calming jar full of slow-moving glitter and sequins. The combination of oil and water is not only a lesson in STEAM (science, technology, engineering, art, and mathematics), it also makes for a nice reminder to slow down every now and then.

MESSY METER

WHAT YOU NEED:

- Tall, empty clear bottles
- Baby oil
- Distilled water
- Food coloring
- Glitter
- Sequins
- Hot glue gun
- Glue sticks
- Super glue (optional)

Continued →

Mindful Jars, continued

1. Fill the bottle ⅓ full with baby oil.

2. Add several drops of food coloring in a color of your choice.

3. Fill the rest of the bottle with distilled water. Add glitter and sequins.

4. With the help of a parent, use hot glue or super glue to glue the lid on the bottle. Allow the glue to dry.

5. Gently turn the bottle up and down. Try taking 10 deep breaths as you watch oil bubbles form in the water.

Painted Rock People

Painted rocks have so many possibilities: paper weights, door stops, or in this case, dolls. Once you pick a theme—monsters, trendy girls, or just random people—all you have to do is paint an array of outfits and costumes. Mix and match faces, hats, shoes, and more. The more options you paint, the more fun the game will be. Bonus points for naming and creating backstories for each new character you create.

MESSY METER

1 2 3 4 5

WHAT YOU NEED:

- Small smooth rocks
- Craft paint
- Paintbrushes
- Permanent markers
- Decoupage medium

Continued →

Painted Rock People, continued

1. Paint your rocks using various colors. If you are going to make people, paint some in skin tone colors for heads. The other rocks for clothing can be any colors you want them to be. Allow the painted rocks to dry completely.

2. On the flesh-toned rocks, add hair and facial features using permanent markers.

3. Embellish the rocks that will act as clothing with polka dots, stripes, and other patterns.

4. Allow the paint to dry. When it's dry, cover the rocks with decoupage medium. This will protect the paint from chipping off.

5. Mix and match rocks to form different characters. Make up stories, paint a background for the rocks to live on, and add some larger rock cars and houses. Go rock crazy!

Tie-Dye Shoes, *page 63*

CRAFTY FASHION

Whether you are an aspiring fashion designer or have been put in charge of making new T-shirts for the baseball team, there is something for everyone in this chapter. There is no need to race out to the store to buy all new things; these projects will have you searching your closet for shirts to ice dye, tote bags to silk screen, and old tennis shoes to make over. You just need a few basic wardrobe DIY skills for endless possibilities. Somebody call the fashion police, you are about to make some noise!

Super Cool Ice Dyeing

This is a new spin on the classic tie-dye technique—no rubber bands or complicated twisting patterns necessary. The ice does all the work for you. No two shirts will ever look the same, and that is why you are going to want an entire closet full.

MESSY METER

1   2   3   4   5

WHAT YOU NEED:

- Pre-washed, 100 percent cotton white T-shirt
- Water
- Cooling rack
- Aluminum pan
- Powdered fabric dye
- Ice

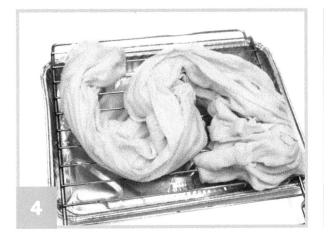

1. Make sure to wash your T-shirt before you begin. Brand-new clothing contains a substance called sizing that will prevent your dye from taking. Also, make sure the shirt is 100 percent cotton to ensure the fibers will dye.

2. Soak your T-shirt in water and wring it out.

3. Place a drying or cooling rack on top of an aluminum pan.

4. Roll up the T-shirt and place it on the rack.

5. Cover the T-shirt with ice. Make sure all the fabric is covered.

Continued →

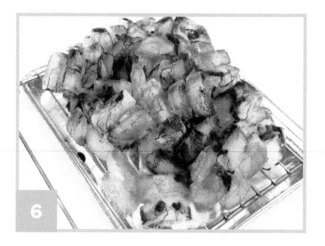

6. Sprinkle the dye powder randomly on top of the ice and wait for the ice to melt.

7. Once all the ice has melted, leave the shirt sitting for another 4 to 6 hours or overnight before washing it by itself in cold water.

8. Your new shirt is ready, and I'm sure now all you can think about is what else you can ice dye. If it's 100 percent cotton, you can dye it: sheets, canvas bags, or even socks!

No-Sew Scrunchies

No one with long hair should find themselves without a scrunchie on hand. Once you learn how to upgrade your standard ponytail holder, you will have a different no-sew scrunchie for every day of the week. Be sure to make extras because your friends are going to want some, too.

MESSY METER

WHAT YOU NEED:

- One 18-inch × 3-inch piece of fabric
- Scissors
- Fabric glue
- 8 inches elastic
- Safety pin

Continued →

WHAT YOU DO:

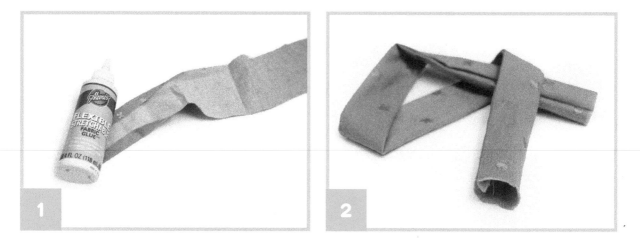

1. Lay the fabric down with the wrong side up. Fold the edge lengthwise and attach with fabric glue. Repeat on the other side to create a glued hem.

2. When the glue is dry, join the two glued edges with more fabric glue to create a long tube. Let it dry.

3. Attach a safety pin to one end of the elastic. Feed it through the tube.

4. When the elastic reaches the other side, remove the safety pin and tie the two ends in a tight knot.

5

5. Add a bit of fabric glue to one of the open ends of cotton fabric and attach it to the other end. This should hide your elastic knot. Allow the glue to dry.

6. Wear No-Sew Scrunchies in your hair, on your wrist, or give them to friends!

Paper Clip and Washi Tape Jewelry

Possibly the easiest jewelry project of all time. These necklaces are so cute you will want one to match every outfit, and you may even want to make a friendship bracelet version for all your friends. You only need two things to make this jewelry, and since washi tape comes in seemingly endless colors and patterns, you could make a new necklace every day.

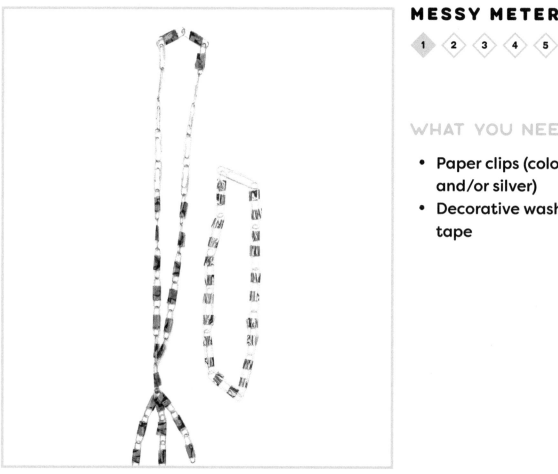

MESSY METER

1 · 2 · 3 · 4 · 5

WHAT YOU NEED:

- Paper clips (colored and/or silver)
- Decorative washi tape

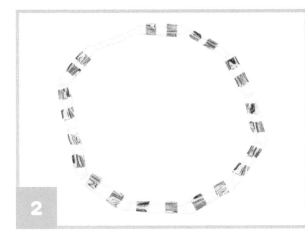

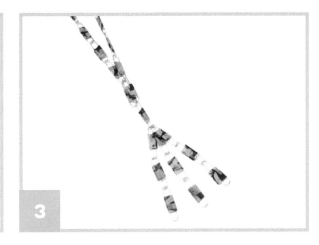

1. Link paper clips together until you reach the right length for a long necklace, bracelet, or choker. Test the length by wrapping the linked paper clips around your neck or wrist to see if you want to make it longer or shorter.

2. Tear off a small piece of washi tape and wrap it around the center of each paper clip. Continue until all but the one that will go on the back of your neck or around your wrist is covered; this one paper clip will act as a clasp.

3. To make a tassel for a necklace, you will need 9 paper clips. Connect 3 paper clips together. Repeat this step until you have 3 sets of 3 linked paper clips. Connect each strand to the center paper clip on the necklace. Cover each paper clip with washi tape and enjoy your new necklace!

QUICK TIP: Can't find the colored paper clips you want? You can always paint them with fingernail polish to customize the look even more.

Faux Sashiko Denim Patches

Have you heard the term "visible mending?" This form of Japanese folk embroidery called *sashiko* involves specific patterns, indigo fabric, and white thread. This project is a stitch-free homage to the original craft. I bet you never knew that a package of iron-on denim patches had so many DIY possibilities.

MESSY METER

1 2 3 4 5

WHAT YOU NEED:

- Package of iron-on denim patches
- Bleach pen
- White paint
- Small, firm paintbrush

QUICK TIP: Don't have a bleach pen handy? You can achieve the same look with white craft paint and a small, stiff paintbrush.

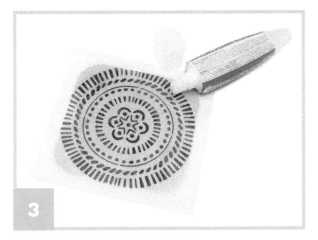

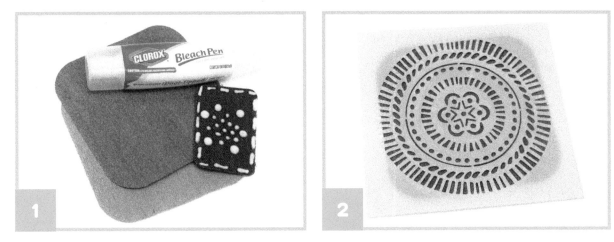

1. Using dark denim iron-on patches will mimic the traditional indigo fabric color. Draw a freehand dot design on the iron-on patch using a bleach pen.

2. You can also use a stencil instead. Place the stencil over the patch and use the bleach pen to "paint" over the stencil.

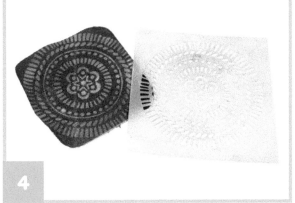

3. Allow the bleach pen to set up overnight. Then, rinse off the bleach and allow the patch to dry.

4. Iron the patch onto jeans, jean jackets, or anything denim.

Pantyhose Silk Screen

Traditional silk screening is a fairly complicated and messy process. Any time you see an image printed on a T-shirt or tote bag, chances are there was a screen with the design burned into it, a large machine, and a lot of paint. Today we are going to DIY our own screens using pantyhose and embroidery hoops.

MESSY METER

1 2 3 4 ⟨5⟩

WHAT YOU NEED:

- Embroidery hoop
- Pantyhose
- Scrap paper or newspaper
- Marker
- Image
- Decoupage medium
- Paintbrush
- Scraping tool
- Paint
- Tote bag or T-shirt

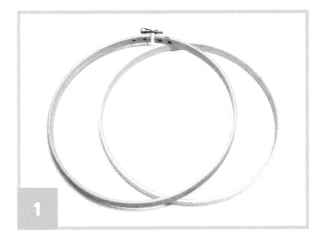

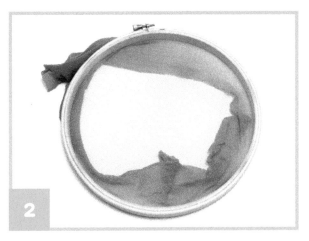

1. Take apart your embroidery hoop. There is one circle inside a slightly larger circle that has a clasp and screw for tightening.

2. Cut off the thigh section from a pair of pantyhose. This will give you a pantyhose tube. Then cut that tube along one side so that you have a rectangle. Stretch the rectangle tightly across the piece of embroidery hoop that does not have any hardware. Place the second ring on top and stretch and pull until the entire circle is covered. Use the screw to tighten and keep the pantyhose in place. There will be excess pantyhose around the edges of the ring and that is OK.

Continued →

Pantyhose Silk Screen, continued

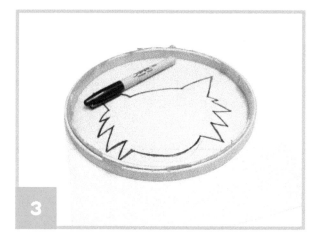

3. Spread out a sheet of paper or newspaper on your work surface. Lay the embroidery hoop on top of the newspaper and draw a simple design using permanent marker. Make sure it's nothing too intricate. Coloring-book pages or silhouettes printed off the internet work great.

4. Paint the area around the image you drew with decoupage medium. You're creating a resist, or a coating, where paint cannot pass through, similar to a stencil. Everywhere there is decoupage medium, the paint will not go through. Apply 2 to 3 coats of the decoupage medium, allowing drying time between each coat, then let it dry completely.

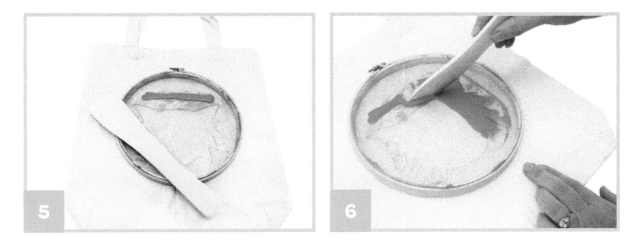

5. Place the hoop on the item you are printing. Make sure the side with the pantyhose touching the surface is face down. Add a bit of paint to the top of the screen.

6. Gently drag the paint across the image using the scraping tool. Make sure all areas of the image are covered in paint.

7. Pull the screen away, rinse it well, and let it dry for a second use.

8. Allow the paint to dry, and leave as-is or embellish with markers and paint pens.

Taco Sunglass Case

Sunglasses banging around in your backpack will get scratched up in no time. Protect them in style with a low-sew felt sunglass case. Once you master the basic idea for this project, anything round is an option. More of a donut guy? Pizza type of gal? If it looks good folded in half, it can be a case for your sunglasses.

MESSY METER

1 2 3 4 5

WHAT YOU NEED:

- 1 sheet each of craft felt in yellow, brown, orange, green, and red (5 sheets total)
- Bowl
- Pen
- Scissors
- Fabric glue
- Needle
- Embroidery floss

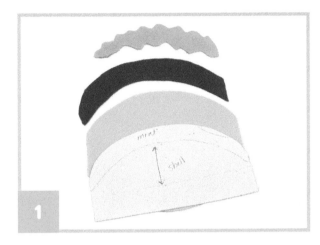

1. Find a bowl with a 10-inch circumference. Use it to trace a circle onto the sheet of yellow felt. Cut out the circle of felt. Use the same bowl to trace a semi-circle onto your brown and green felt. Trim the green felt into a wavy pattern.

2. Glue the brown and green felt to one side of the taco shell. Allow glue to dry.

Continued →

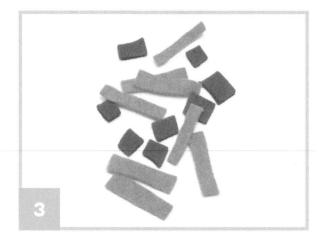

3

4

3. Cut small strips of red and orange felt to be the cheese and tomatoes.

4. Fold the taco in half and sew the two sides together using a needle and embroidery floss. Completely close one end of the semicircle and leave one end open with a hole large enough to insert your sunglasses. Glue the cheese and tomatoes onto the taco.

5. When the glue has dried, your felt sunglass case is ready for action! That was so easy you might just make one for each of your favorite round foods: pancakes, oranges, and bagels, here you come!

Tie-Dye Shoes

Customize your kicks with this fun faux tie-dye project. In just an afternoon, you could have the coolest shoes in school. The combination of permanent markers and rubbing alcohol is part science experiment, part DIY fashion project. Go for bright colors, stick with blues and purples for a galaxy look, or experiment with your favorite sports teams' colors.

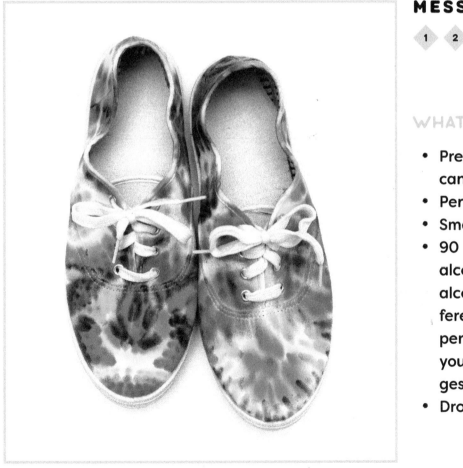

MESSY METER

1 2 3 4 5

WHAT YOU NEED:

- Prewashed canvas shoes
- Permanent markers
- Small spray bottle
- 90 percent rubbing alcohol (rubbing alcohol comes in different concentration percentages, and you need the strongest you can find)
- Drop cloth (optional)

Continued →

Tie-Dye Shoes, continued

1. Make sure your shoes are pre-washed in the washing machine. New clothing and shoes come treated with a substance called sizing, which can prevent dye, or in this case permanent markers, from adhering.

2. Remove the laces. Use your markers to make dots all over the canvas part of the shoes. There is no right or wrong placement for colors and dots, but be aware that if you put blue dots next to yellow dots, green will appear between them.

3. Fill the spray bottle with rubbing alcohol. Place the shoes on a drop cloth or go outside. Spray the shoes. The colors will start to bleed into a tie-dye pattern almost immediately. Continue spraying until you have the look you want. Allow the shoes to dry.

4. Once the alcohol has dried, you can put your laces back in and wear your new shoes. Prepare yourself for plenty of compliments and pats on the back. If you wash your shoes again, be sure to wash them separately.

Shrink Plastic Flair ◆

With clear, plastic shrink film sheets, you can trace almost any image or draw something yourself that can then be shrunken down into wearable flair. Coloring book pages, your school logo, illustrations from magazines—when you trace an image onto shrink film, all things are possible. Shrink film is just as much fun to make and wear as it is to watch shrink in the oven.

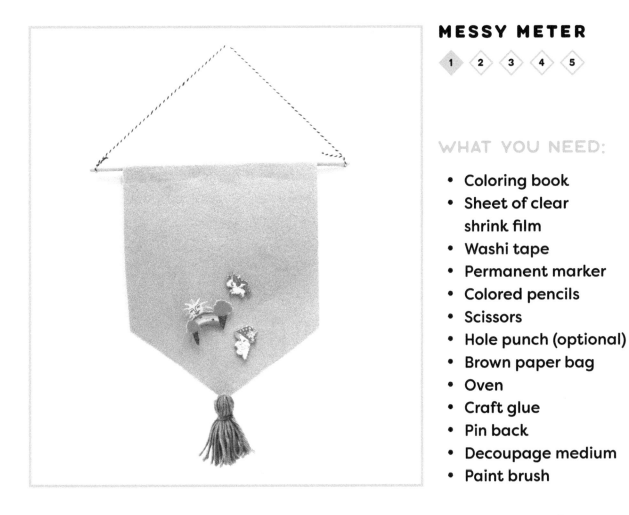

MESSY METER

1 2 3 4 5

WHAT YOU NEED:

- Coloring book
- Sheet of clear shrink film
- Washi tape
- Permanent marker
- Colored pencils
- Scissors
- Hole punch (optional)
- Brown paper bag
- Oven
- Craft glue
- Pin back
- Decoupage medium
- Paint brush

Continued →

Shrink Plastic Flair, continued

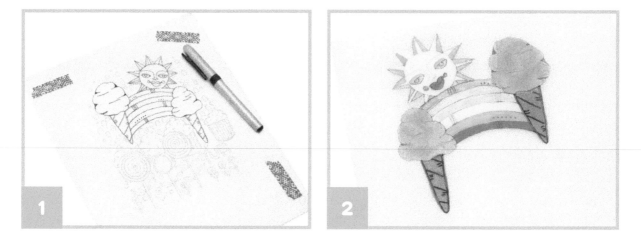

1. Select a coloring book page and lay the sheet of shrink film on top. Secure the pages together with washi tape. Trace the image onto the shrink film using a permanent marker. Remember that your image will shrink by ⅓ when it is heated.

2. Color in the image with colored pencils. Next, cut out the image. If you plan to hang this as a charm instead of using it as a pin, now is the time to make a hole with a hole punch.

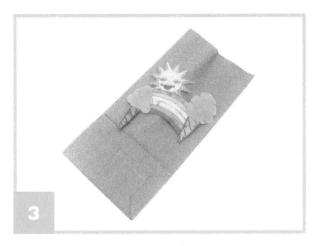

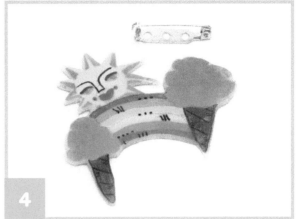

3. Ask an adult for help baking the film in the oven according to the manufacturer's instructions. Different brands of shrink film have different instructions—you may be asked to first place your design on a brown paper bag. Remember to always ask an adult for help when working with the oven.

4. The image will shrink and thicken in the oven. Allow it to cool completely. Attach the pin back with craft glue. A layer of decoupage medium can also be added as a protective top coat and to add shine.

5. Once the glue is completely dry, pin your creation to your jacket or back-pack and get your flair on!

Tassel Key Chains

How do you find your backpack amid the crowd of bags lining the hooks in your school halls? You add a bit of DIY dazzle. Tassels could not be easier to make and once you learn how, no backpack, zipper pull, or key chain will be safe again.

WHAT YOU NEED:

- **Embroidery floss**
- **Cardboard**
- **Scissors**
- **Wooden beads**
- **Pom-poms**
- **Large-eyed sewing needle**
- **Split ring**

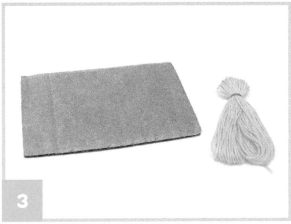

1. First, use a piece of cardboard to create your tassel. The width of the cardboard will determine the length of the tassel. Cut the cardboard to your desired tassel length.

2. Wrap an entire skein of embroidery floss around the cardboard, or make 100 passes.

3. Slide the embroidery floss off the cardboard. Tie off the top half inch with another piece of floss and tie a knot.

Continued →

Tassel Key Chains, continued

4. With a pair of scissors, cut the loops on the long end of the tassel.

5. Attach another double strand of embroidery floss to a split ring. Thread the sewing needle with the floss and go through the pom-poms and beads.

6. Loop your needle through the top of the tassel and tie off in a knot.

7. Mix and match floss for multicolored tassels, paint your beads—make your own pom-poms, too.

Sticker Resist T-Shirt

Foam stickers are about to be your new best fashion-forward friends. They come in so many precut shapes and sizes, plus you can buy sheets of sticky-back craft foam and make your own designs. In this case it does not matter what is printed on your sticker, as it will be acting as a resist. What matters is the shape of the sticker.

MESSY METER

WHAT YOU NEED:

- Prewashed white T-shirt
- Foam craft stickers
- Sheet of sticky-back craft foam (optional)
- Fabric spray paint
- Drop cloth (optional)

Continued →

Sticker Resist T-Shirt, continued

1. Gather foam stickers in fun shapes or use a sheet of craft foam to cut some of your own.

2. Cover the shirt with stickers. Make sure to leave space in between each sticker.

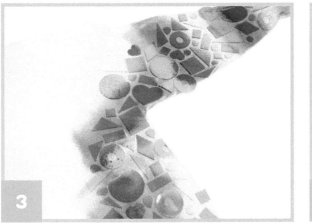

3. Take the shirt outside and lay it on the grass or a drop cloth. Spray the paint over the area with stickers. Allow the paint to dry.

4. Remove and discard stickers to reveal your design. Try out different patterns and sticker shapes.

Soap Pops, *page 76*

GIFT IDEAS

Ever heard the saying, "It is better to give than it is to receive"? That goes double when it comes to handmade gifts. You will have so much fun making soap pops and clay donuts, you'll want to make two of everything so you can keep one for yourself. One trinket jar for your cousin, three for your desk. Trust us, go ahead and gather the supplies to make more than one. You will thank us later!

Soap Pops ◈

No one will ever have to tell you twice to wash your hands with soap this cute. Soap making is an easy process once you get the hang of things. You can use all kinds of colors, molds, and scents, but this project calls for a Popsicle mold. These soap pops will look cute enough to eat, but we strongly advise against it. Steps 3 through 5 need to be done in a timely manner before the soap begins to cool and harden. Work quickly, but be careful with the hot soap.

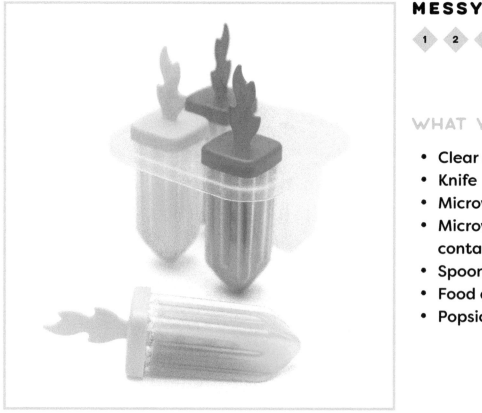

MESSY METER

◆ 1   ◆ 2   ◆ 3   ◆ 4   ◆ 5

WHAT YOU NEED:

- Clear glycerin soap
- Knife
- Microwave
- Microwave-safe container
- Spoon
- Food coloring
- Popsicle mold

1. Glycerin soap usually comes in a large slab. Ask an adult to help cut it into cubes.

2. Place the cubes in a microwave-safe container.

3. Microwave the soap for 30 seconds. Remove and stir. If it is not melted, microwave for 15 seconds.

4. Add a few drops of food coloring or soap colorant.

Continued →

Soap Pops, continued

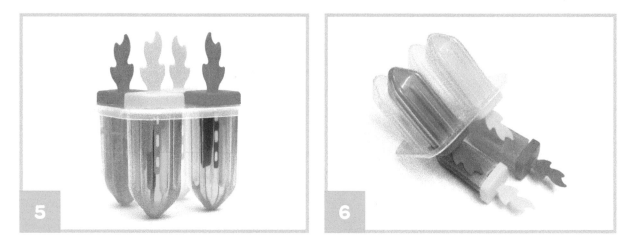

5. Pour liquid soap into the mold. Add a stick. Repeat for each color until the mold is full.

6. Allow soap to cool and harden for about an hour. Put in the freezer for the last 10 minutes for extra easy removal.

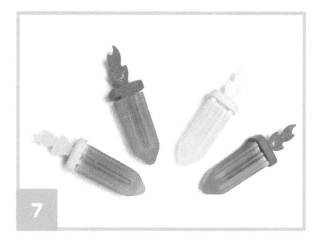

7. Use the soap pop like any other type of bar soap. When it's all gone, you can use the mold to make another batch!

T-Shirt Notebook ◈

Outgrown your favorite T-shirt? Want to help a friend always remember summer camp? Does last year's class shirt have a stain? You can recycle that old sentimental T-shirt into a new notebook cover. Perfect for school, journaling, or as a gift.

MESSY METER

1 2 3 4 5

WHAT YOU NEED:

- Old T-shirt
- Blank notebook
- Scissors
- Spray craft glue
- Craft glue
- 2 sheets of felt (approximately the same size as the notebook cover)

Continued →

T-Shirt Notebook, **continued**

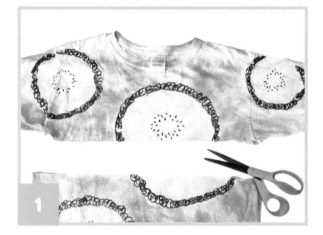

1. Cut off the top half of the shirt at the underarms. Discard the top.

2. You now have a tube of T-shirt. Cut along one edge to open the fabric.

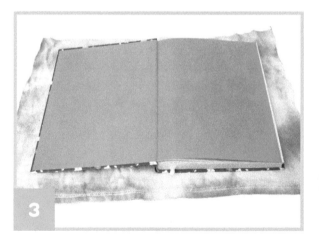

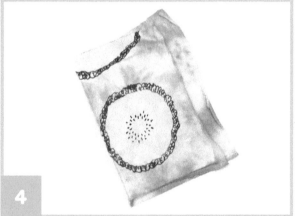

3. Measure about an inch of material all the way around the edge of the notebook and trim any excess.

4. Ask an adult to go outside to spray the front and back covers with spray craft glue. Lay out the T-shirt rectangle and place the notebook on top. Smooth out any air bubbles.

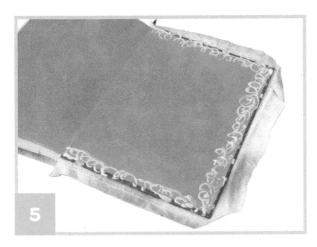

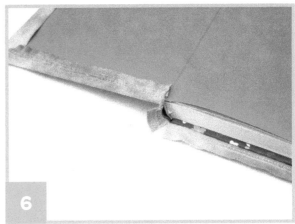

5. Now that the fabric is attached to the outside of the journal, it is time to finish the inside. Cut all four corners of the fabric and cut two slits in the fabric at the spine of the journal. On the inside cover, add craft glue about 1 inch from the edge on three sides of the journal (you don't need glue on the "gutter," or the inside edge, of the journal).

6. Fold the edges of the T-shirt in and smooth onto the inside journal cover. Repeat steps 5 and 6 on the inside back cover. The tabs created from the two slits you cut at the spine will be all that is left unglued.

Continued →

T-Shirt Notebook, continued

7. Cut a sheet of craft felt to be slightly smaller than the covers of the notebook. Glue the felt to the inside of the front and back covers to hide the raw edges of the T-shirt.

8. To hide the small tabs at the spine of the notebook, add craft glue to the tab and roll the fabric up towards the pages. There should be a slight lip in the top and bottom of the notebook's spine where the rolled tab can be glued in place. Allow all the glue to dry.

9. Once all the glue is dry, your notebook is ready to be gifted. That is, if you can bear to part with it.

Stitched Greeting Cards

Whether you have a pen pal or you owe your grandmother a thank-you note, these stitched cards are a fun way to spice up snail mail. When is the last time you got an actual letter in the mail? How fun would it be to not only get a letter, but a stitched one at that? You can create your own design to stitch or embellish a card already in your collection.

MESSY METER

1 2 3 4 5

WHAT YOU NEED:

- Blank cards
- Craft paint
- Paintbrush
- Embroidery needle
- Embroidery floss
- Ruler
- Tape
- Decorative paper
- Glue stick

Continued →

Stitched Greeting Cards, continued

1. Paint fun images on the blank cards with craft paint. Allow paint to dry. If you'd rather not paint an image, use a card that already has a design on it.

2. Decide what parts of your card you would like to stitch. Using an embroidery needle, pierce holes into the card approximately ¼ inch apart.

3. Measure and cut approximately 12 inches of embroidery floss. Thread your needle and make a knot at the end, leaving a tail about 1 inch long, and tape it to the inside of the card.

4. Starting from the inside of the card push your needle through the first hole.

5. Pull the thread until the knot will not allow you to pull any further.

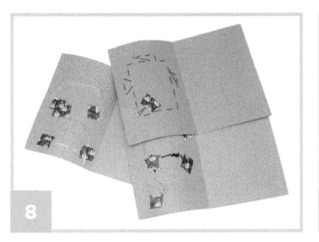

6. Push your needle into the next hole, working from the front to the inside of your card, and pull until you can't pull the thread any further. You have made your first stitch.

7. Repeat steps 4 through 6 on the next hole. This is called a running stitch, which is a simple in-and-out stitch.

8. When you reach the end of your design, cut the embroidery thread off the needle and tape the end of the thread inside of the card. Make sure all loose ends are taped down well.

9. Cut a piece of felt slightly smaller than the inside of the card. Glue the felt to the inside of the card to cover the back of your stitches.

10. Write your letter, create a card set as a gift, or present your friend with the fanciest custom gift card holder ever.

Best Friend Doughnut Charm Necklaces ◆❗

These doughnut charms are so sweet that they look good enough to eat. It may be hard to part with this necklace as a gift, so feel free to make a baker's dozen.

WHAT YOU NEED:

- Polymer clay in tan and assorted colors for frosting and sprinkles
- Various clay tools (optional)
- Aluminum foil
- Oven
- Necklace chain
- Small blank flat circle charm tag
- Craft glue
- Super glue

1. Roll a small amount of tan clay into a ball. Pinch off another color for the icing and roll that into a smaller ball.

2. Gently flatten the tan ball so that it starts to look like the shape of a doughnut.

3. Flatten the clay for the icing. Use a pinching motion around the edge to shape it into a flattened flower shape.

4. Press the icing onto the doughnut. Using a clay tool or an unsharpened pencil, make a hole in the center.

Continued →

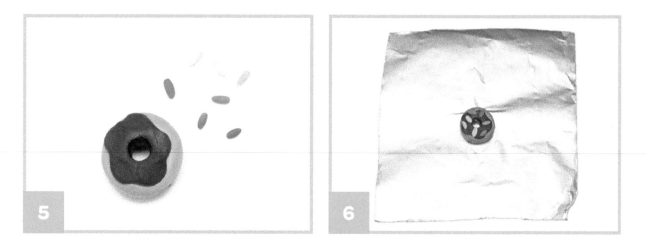

5. Roll out little sprinkles with tiny amounts of colorful clay. This is just like rolling a snake with play dough except much smaller and between your thumb and finger.

6. Gently press the sprinkles onto the donut in a random pattern. Place your doughnut on a piece of aluminum foil and bake according to the manufacturer's directions. Each brand of polymer clay has a different set of instructions for baking times and temperatures.

7. Remove from oven and allow to cool completely.

8. Once the charm is completely cool, ask an adult for help to super glue the doughnut onto the small flat circle charm tag. Allow this to dry completely.

9. Thread the circle charm tag onto the necklace chain. Your charm necklace is ready for gifting.

Rainbow Bath Bombs

Who wouldn't want to receive bath bombs as a gift? They're fun, they fizz, and they turn your bath water a fun color. Make sure to whip up a double batch because everyone who invites you to their parties will be hoping you gift them with some homemade bath bombs.

MESSY METER

1 2 3 4 5

WHAT YOU NEED:

- Mixing bowl
- Spoon
- ½ cup cornstarch
- ½ cup citric acid
- 1 cup baking soda
- ½ cup Epsom salt
- 2 tbsp coconut oil
- Microwave-safe mug or bowl
- Food coloring
- Witch hazel
- 5 disposable cups
- Cooking spray
- Bath bomb molds
- Cellophane (optional)
- Ribbon (optional)

1. Combine the cornstarch, citric acid, baking soda, and Epsom salt in a mixing bowl and mix well. Microwave 2 tablespoons of coconut oil in a mug or bowl for 10 seconds to get it to a liquid state.

2. Add the coconut oil to the dry ingredients and mix well. Divide the mixture into 5 disposable cups. Add food coloring to each cup.

Continued →

3. Mix in food coloring well. Ingredients should have the consistency of sand that's perfect for castle building: not too wet, but not too dry. If the mixture feels a little dry, add one or two drops of witch hazel at a time until it's just right.

4. Spray the inside of a bath bomb mold with cooking spray. Fill the mold with the colored mixtures in various layers. Remember you will see the edges of the bath bomb so push the different colors to the walls of the mold to be sure you see the different colored layers.

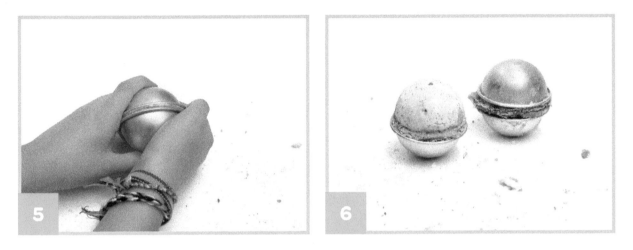

5. Slightly overfill both sides of the bath bomb mold. Take the two sides and press them together firmly. Let the mold sit for 24 hours.

6. Very gently pull off one side of the mold. If the mixture is still sticking to the mold, press the two sides back together and try putting it in the freezer for an hour.

7. Your bath bombs should be hard enough for you to wrap them up in some cellophane, put a bow on top, and bring them to your next party.

Paper Bag Hanging Stars, *page 121*

DIY DÉCOR IDEAS

Your room should be a reflection of you and your style. Unleash your inner decorator with a few easy room accents you can make yourself, like no-sew pillows, wall hangings, and clay dishes for your jewelry. Over the course of a weekend your room could get a total DIY makeover.

Drip Pots

At first glance this colorful project might look like a major mess waiting to happen, but actually cleanup is a breeze. For once you get to spill paint on purpose.

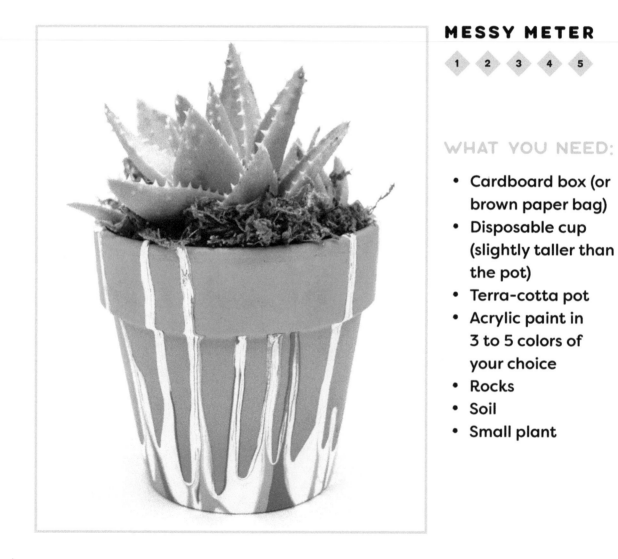

MESSY METER

1　2　3　4　5

WHAT YOU NEED:

- Cardboard box (or brown paper bag)
- Disposable cup (slightly taller than the pot)
- Terra-cotta pot
- Acrylic paint in 3 to 5 colors of your choice
- Rocks
- Soil
- Small plant

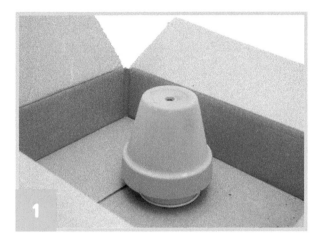

1. Place a cardboard box or a brown paper bag on a table. This will be your work surface. Place the disposable cup upside down and then place the terra-cotta pot upside down over the cup. You will be pouring paint onto the bottom of the pot, and since the disposable cup is taller than the terra-cotta pot, the rim of the pot will not touch the box. This will prevent paint from causing the pot to stick to the box.

2. Squeeze a line of paint along the edge of the pot bottom so that the paint begins to drip down the sides.

Continued →

Drip Pots, continued

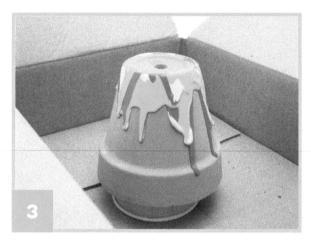

3. Add the next color directly on top of the first. The weight of the paint will start to create a natural drip pattern.

4. Once you have applied all of the colors you can go back and apply a second round. The trick is to not add so much paint that you can't see the original pot underneath. Allow paint to dry completely. Discard the cup and box.

5. Line the bottom of the pot with a few rocks and then add soil. Plant a small plant or flower.

No-Sew Felt Pillow

No sewing skills are necessary to make a bed full of custom throw pillows! Craft felt comes in so many colors and patterns you will be able to make yourself a new pillow for every day of the week. We will be gluing instead of sewing, so grab yourself a bottle of the sticky stuff and let's get crafty.

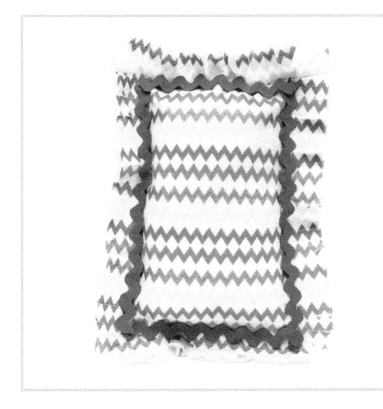

MESSY METER

WHAT YOU NEED:

- 2 sheets of craft felt (make sure they are the same size)
- Ruler
- Pen
- Scissors
- Craft glue
- Clothespins
- Polyester fiber fill
- Rickrack (optional)

Continued →

WHAT YOU DO:

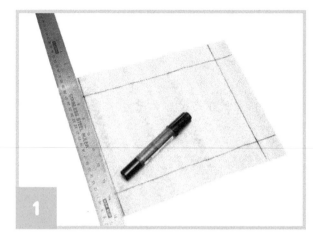

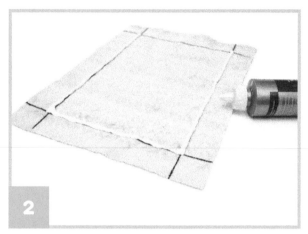

1. Craft felt comes in sheets at the store. Make sure to choose two sheets that are the same size, and they can be any color or pattern of your choosing. Measure a 2-inch border around all four sides of one sheet of felt and mark it with a pen.

2. Lay the sheet of felt on a flat surface with the pen marks facing up. Apply a thick line of glue on three of the four lines you measured. Be sure not to do all four sides! Place the second sheet of felt on top of the one with glue, taking care to line up all the edges. Press down firmly and allow the glue to dry overnight.

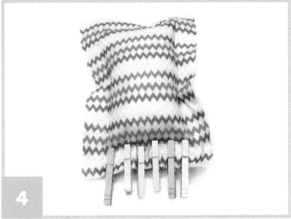

3. Once the glue is dry you will have a felt pouch. Use the polyester fiber fill to stuff the pouch up to the point of the marked line.

4. Add a thick line of glue along the last line inside the pillow. This will close the pillow up. Now that the pillow is puffy and full of stuffing the two pieces of felt will be harder to close and make contact with the glue. This is where the clothespins come in, to make sure there is good contact between the two pieces of felt. Allow the glue to dry overnight.

Continued →

5. Your pillow is almost ready! Remove the clothespins. Cut slits in the border of felt approximately 1 inch apart to create a fringed border. Be sure to stop cutting right before the glue line begins. Feel free to trim your pillow with glue and rickrack.

6. Use your new pillows on the bed, in a chair, or keep one in the car for road-trip naps. Spot clean when needed.

Embroidery Hoop Wall Pocket

You can never have too many places to put all those papers you bring home from school, pictures of friends, or cards you want to hang onto. Table top surface for storage in your room might be sparse, so this is why you need to think about hanging things. Allow me to introduce you to these easy DIY wall pockets.

Continued →

MESSY METER

1 2 3 4 5

WHAT YOU NEED:

- Embroidery hoop
- Fabric (in a size larger than the embroidery hoop)
- Scissors
- Hot glue gun
- Glue sticks
- 1 sheet of craft felt (in a width larger than the embroidery hoop)

Embroidery Hoop Wall Pocket, continued

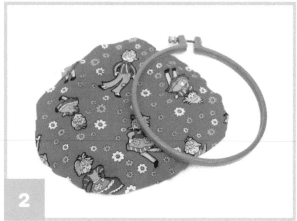

1. Embroidery hoops consist of two parts: one hoop with the tightening hardware and one without it.

2. Place your fabric across the hoop without any hardware.

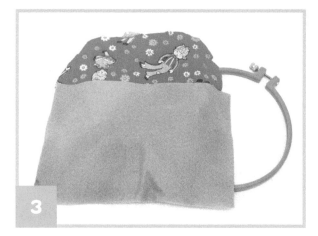

3. Halfway across the fabric place a sheet of craft felt. This will be the pocket.

4. Place the second hoop with the hardware over the plain hoop and fabric.

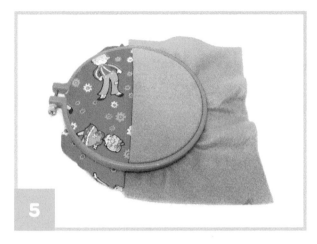 

5. Tighten the hardware on the hoop while pulling both the craft felt and fabric taut.

6. Trim off excess fabric on the back of the wall pocket. Ask an adult for help to add hot glue around the edges and hold your fabric in place.

7. Hang on the wall and use your handy dandy new pocket!

Easy Woven Wall Hanging

Ever heard of macramé? This is a complicated craft that uses knotted rope patterns to create amazing and intricate designs, often hung on the wall. Today we are going to make our own faux macramé woven wall hanging. Same groovy effect, but much less tricky.

MESSY METER

1 2 3 4 5

WHAT YOU NEED:

- Wooden hoop (diameter depends on how large you want your wall hanging)
- Chunky yarn (your choice of colors cut into 2-foot lengths)
- Scissors

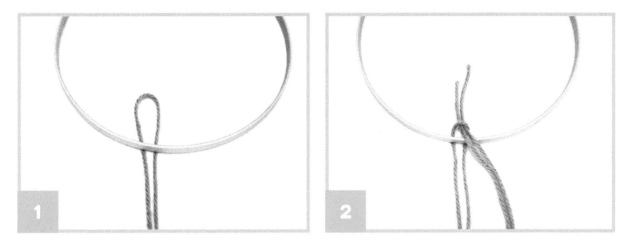

1. Take one length of yarn and fold it in half. Place the piece of yarn behind the hoop on a flat surface.

2. Bring the tails of the yarn up and put them through the loop of yarn.

Continued →

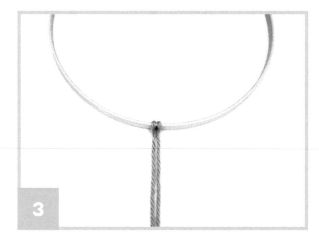

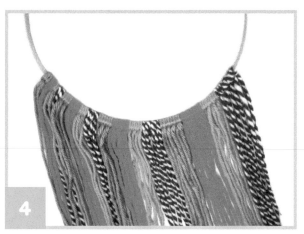

3. Pull the tail until the yarn tightens around the hoop. This is called a Lark's Head Knot.

4. How many strands of yarn you add or in what pattern is completely up to you. Remember, with a hoop you can only arrange the yarn to go a little less than halfway up the sides of the hoop in order for the strands to hang flat.

5. Trim the ends of the yarn with scissors, and try making a stylish angle. Hang on your wall with a pushpin!

No-Sew Felt Enamel Pin Banner ◆

Your collection of enamel pins and round buttons has gotten so out of control you can't fit them all on your jacket anymore. We use jewelry boxes because we don't wear all our rings or necklaces at once, right? Why not make a hanging display for your flair? This way you can appreciate all the fun designs you've collected when you are not wearing them.

MESSY METER

1　2　3　4　5

WHAT YOU NEED:

- One 9-inch × 12-inch sheet of stiffened craft felt
- Scissors
- Hot glue gun
- Glue stick
- One 1-foot wooden dowel
- Bakers twine
- Tassel

Continued →

No-Sew Felt Enamel Pin Banner, continued

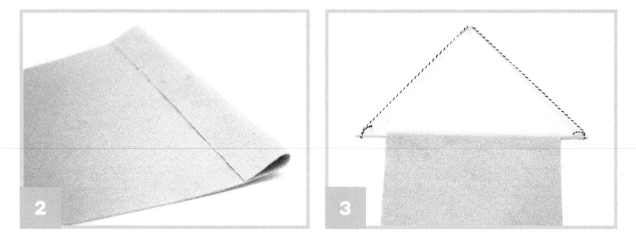

1. Cut a triangle shape in the bottom of one side of the stiffened craft felt.

2. Lay the dowel across the other end of the felt. Roll the edge of the felt over the dowel and using a hot glue gun attach to felt. This should make a small round channel for the dowel.

3. Insert the dowel. Tie a 24-inch length of bakers twine to the ends of the dowel. This will be how you hang the banner.

4. Use a hot glue gun to attach a tassel to the tip of the triangle.

5. Hang up and display all of those pins in your collection.

Cookie Cutter Ring Dishes

Air-dry clay will have you feeling like a regular ceramics artist in no time. No baking necessary to make a slew of cute trinket dishes. Paper clips, spare change, and jewelry will now always have a place to land when you have a room full of these handy cuties. This project involves a surprising tool, too: cookie cutters!

MESSY METER

1 2 3 4 5

WHAT YOU NEED:

- Air-dry clay
- Cutting board or wax paper
- Rolling pin
- Cookie cutter
- Disposable cups
- Craft paint
- Paintbrushes
- Decoupage medium
- Sponge brush

Continued →

Cookie Cutter Ring Dishes, continued

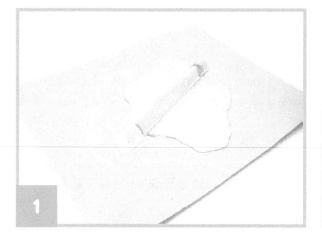

1. Roll out air dry clay on a cutting board or wax paper. Remember that anything you use for crafting—cookie cutters, cutting boards, or rolling pins—can no longer be used on food.

2. Press cookie cutters down firmly into the clay. Cookie cutters with a wide design that will lend itself to being formed into a dish will work best.

3. Lift the cut clay and place it on top of a disposable cup so that the clay bends inwards at the edges to form a dish. Let dry overnight.

4. When the clay is dry, use craft paint in various colors to decorate the dishes. Don't forget to paint the edges and underside. Allow the paint to dry completely.

5. Using a sponge brush, apply a layer of decoupage medium as a protective top coat. Let dry completely.

Melty Bead Picture Frame ◆

Want a way to forever remember that camping trip you took with your Scout troop? Maybe your favorite family photo pinned to the cork board deserves a little something extra? Enter your new melty bead picture frame. That's right, these tiny beads can make up a design that is as complicated or basic as you want. Once you have the pattern you want, all you have to do is iron it and it is forever a frame.

MESSY METER

1   2   3   4   5

WHAT YOU NEED:

- Photo
- Large melty bead pegboard
- Melty beads in a variety of colors
- Parchment paper
- Iron
- Cardboard
- Scissors
- Craft glue
- String

WHAT YOU DO:

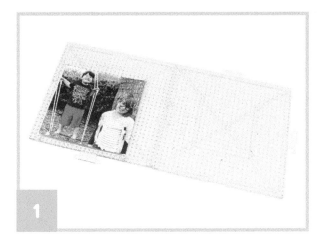

1

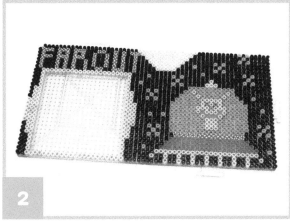

2

1. Since this is going to be a picture frame, the first thing you want to do is choose what size photo you will be using and be sure to leave that area blank on the pegboard.

2. Once you have the space for your photograph reserved, fill in the rest of the pegboard with melty beads in the design of your choice.

Continued →

Melty Bead Picture Frame, continued

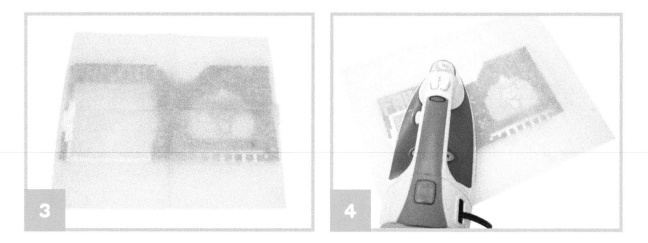

3. When you are finished arranging the beads, gently place a sheet of parchment paper on top of the design. This will protect your iron from getting any melted plastic on it.

4. Ask an adult to help iron the melty beads according to the manufacturer's instructions. Medium heat with a constantly moving iron is always a safe bet.

5. Allow the beads to cool, and then remove the design from the pegboard. Cut a piece of cardboard the same size as your design. This will act as the back of your picture frame. Glue the cardboard to the back side of the frame and leave the top edge open where the picture will be inserted.

6. Glue a piece of string to the back so you can hang your picture. Slide your photo through the spot where you did not glue the frame to the cardboard.

7. Hang your new, totally far-out picture frame.

Wrapped Desk Caddy

Cotton laundry cording is an unlikely craft supply, but it works so well on so many different fun projects. The cording is 100 percent cotton, which means you can paint it, dye it, and use it like a blank canvas. In this project we are going to upgrade a plain wooden storage bin into something better. Get ready to get your polka dot on!

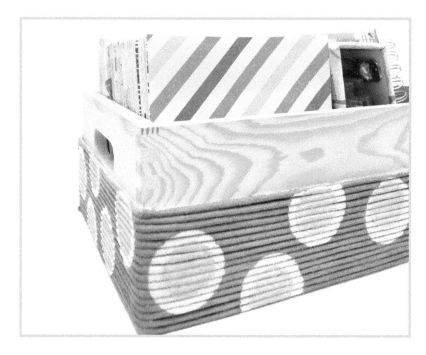

MESSY METER

WHAT YOU NEED:

- Wooden crate
- Craft glue
- Cotton laundry cording
- Scissors
- Large round punch
- Sticky-back craft foam sheets
- Craft paint
- Round sponge dauber

1. Starting at the bottom of the crate, apply a section of glue. Attach the cording to the glue and wind it around the crate.

2. Continue until you have covered as much of the crate as you want. Allow glue to dry completely.

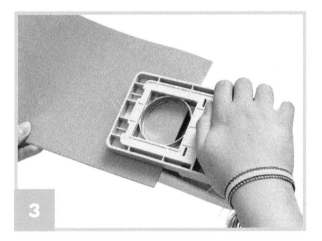

3. Use a craft punch or scissors to make circles from the craft foam.

Continued →

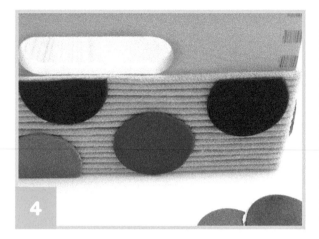

4. Firmly attach the stickers to the rope in a random pattern. You can cut some in half for the edges.

5. Paint all of the laundry cording with craft paint. Allow paint to dry completely.

6. Remove and discard the stickers to reveal white polka dots. Use a round sponge dauber to make accent polka dots. Allow paint to dry completely.

7. Use your new bin for art supplies, random papers, or other knickknacks to keep your desk organized.

Paper Bag Hanging Stars

Every day can feel like a party when you make a batch of these paper bag stars. Whether you use colorful gift bags or paint your own brown bags, they are guaranteed to liven up your space. The best part is they look super fancy and complicated, but they are actually ridiculously easy to make.

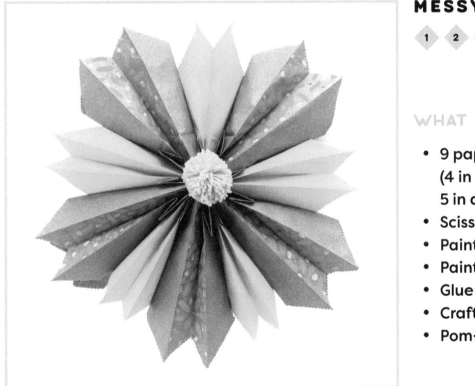

MESSY METER

1 2 3 4 5

WHAT YOU NEED:

- 9 paper bags (4 in one size and 5 in a smaller size)
- Scissors
- Paint
- Paintbrush
- Glue stick
- Craft glue
- Pom-pom

Continued →

Paper Bag Hanging Stars, continued

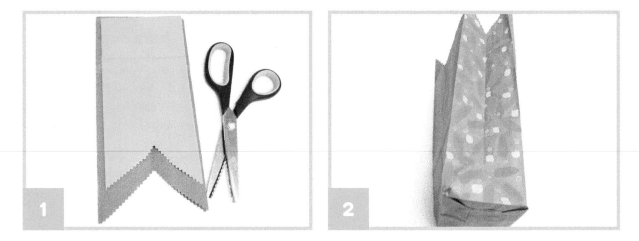

1. Cut out a triangle from the open end of each bag. Scissors with decorative edges are fun to use, too.

2. Paint the bags if you would like. (The sides will be the most visible part.) Allow the painted bags to dry.

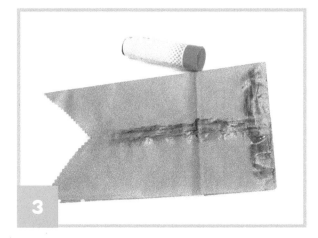

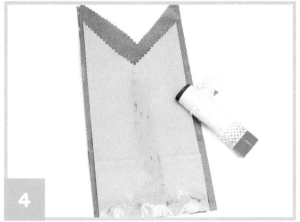

3. Fold the bags back to their original shape. Use a glue stick to make a T shape on one side of the bag.

4. Place the next bag on top of the first, gluing them together. On the second bag add another T of glue.

5. Repeat until all 9 bags are connected. Fan the bags out and you will start to see your star forming. In order to connect the last bag to the first, you can use a glue stick or craft glue.

6. Add a pom-pom with craft glue to the center of the star where all the bags meet. Allow the glue to dry completely.

7. When you are done you can hang your stars on the wall with a push pin or glue some string inside one of the bags to hang the stars from the ceiling. Have fun making your own paper bag galaxy.

Groovy Gravel Trays

This project is as easy as 1-2-3 because there are literally 3 steps. Now that's what I call an easy craft project. No dish or tray will ever be safe with you again after you learn this trick. You will be making a set for yourself and for your friends. Try using glitter, gravel, or seed beads!

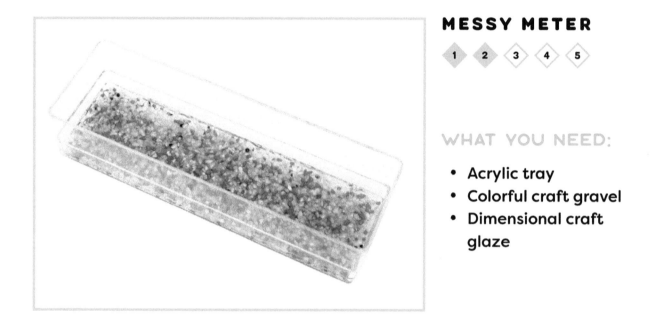

MESSY METER

1   2   3   4   5

WHAT YOU NEED:

- Acrylic tray
- Colorful craft gravel
- Dimensional craft glaze

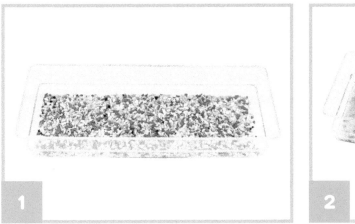

1

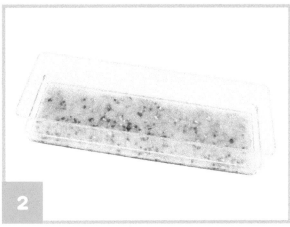

2

1. Sprinkle a shallow layer of gravel in the bottom of the dish. Make sure the layer is as even as possible.

2. Pour a dimensional craft glaze, like a thick decoupage medium, over the gravel. Gently agitate the tray to be sure the glaze reaches to the bottom and to let any air bubbles rise to the surface. Look for any bubbles and pop them. Allow the glaze to dry completely.

3. Your new tray is ready to go after about 24 hours!

> **NOTE:** Once you've used a dish or a tray to make these acrylic trays, they are no longer food safe.

Petite Pom-Pom Rug

Bet you never thought you would be able to tell your friends you made your own accent rug. Well, you can! Once you master making pom-poms, the options for décor are endless and include accent rugs. Put this cutie right beside your bed so your footsies never again have to touch a cold floor first thing in the morning.

MESSY METER

1 **2** 3 4 5

WHAT YOU NEED:

- Yarn
- Scissors
- Cardboard
- Rug canvas

1. Make a few dozen medium to large yarn pom-poms. See the sidebar on the next page for full instructions.

2. Attach pom-poms to the rug canvas. Remember, this is a small accent rug, so you don't need a huge piece.

3. Flip the rug back over and trim off excess canvas.

Continued →

DIY POM-POMS

Pom-poms are one of the best crafts ever invented. They take almost every project to the next level. You can wear them, decorate your room with them, and put them on gifts to accent your wrapping. I've yet to find something that would not be made better by adding a pom-pom (or two).

WHAT YOU NEED:

- One 6-inch × 4-inch piece of cardboard
- Scissors
- Yarn

WHAT YOU DO:

1. Wrap your yarn around the 4-inch section of the cardboard 125 times. You can start by holding down the tail of yarn and wrapping over it. Remember: the wider the cardboard, the bigger the pom-pom. Also, the more times you wrap the yarn around the cardboard, the fluffier your pom-pom will be.

2. When you have finished wrapping, cut your yarn. Gently slide your yarn bundle off the cardboard.

3. Use a 6-inch length of yarn to tie a knot around the center of the bundle. Pull the yarn tight so that the bundle cinches in the middle. Tie a second knot so the first knot doesn't come loose.

4. Cut open the loops on either side of the pom-pom. Make sure to not cut the piece of yarn tied around the center. You will use this to tie the pom-pom to the canvas.

5. Trim any stray edges of the pom-pom so that all the strands look uniform in length.

Recycled Wrapped Vase, *page 132*

CRAFTING WITH NATURE AND CRAFTY UPCYCLES

Nature provides us with endless arts-and-crafts opportunities. You can make dyes with flowers and herbs, press small bouquets into keepsakes, and with a little paint, fallen acorns become wee characters. Crafting with nature also teaches us to make use of what we have. Before you throw that cardboard paper towel roll or magazine in the bin, think to yourself how it could instead be transformed into something entirely new. One person's trash is another person's craft project. Once you get inspired by the projects in this chapter, you will be combing your backyard and dumpster diving for craft supplies in no time.

Recycled Wrapped Vase

A shiny glass vase full of flowers is overrated. Give me a bouquet of sticks and pom-poms in a recycled colorful yarn-wrapped vase any day.

MESSY METER

1   2   3   4   5

WHAT YOU NEED:

- Empty jar
- Craft glue
- Yarn in a variety of colors
- Sticks
- Pom-poms

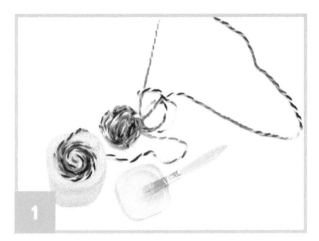

1. At the bottom of the jar, apply a section of glue. Attach yarn to the glue and coil it around the jar.

2. Repeat this process, working one section at a time, until the entire vase is covered.

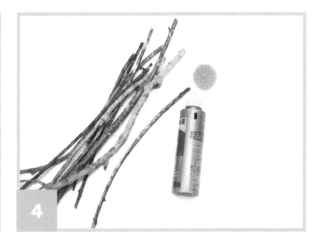

3. When you are finished, cut off the excess yarn and glue the remaining yarn tail inside the vase.

4. Make a bouquet of pom-pom flowers (see page 128) by gluing pom-poms to sticks. Fill the vase with the bouquet.

Continued →

MINI POM-POMS

For every color and size of pom-pom you have ever seen, there are probably an equal number of methods for making them. This fun option gives you perfect "bite-size" pom-poms every time.

WHAT YOU NEED:

- Yarn
- Fork
- Scissors
- Ruler

WHAT YOU DO:

1. Use a fork where the tines stay the same width apart the full length of the tines. Wrap yarn around the tines, leaving a 3-inch tail. Wrap the yarn a second time around, covering the tail, which will secure it.

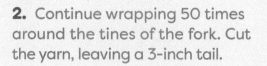

2. Continue wrapping 50 times around the tines of the fork. Cut the yarn, leaving a 3-inch tail.

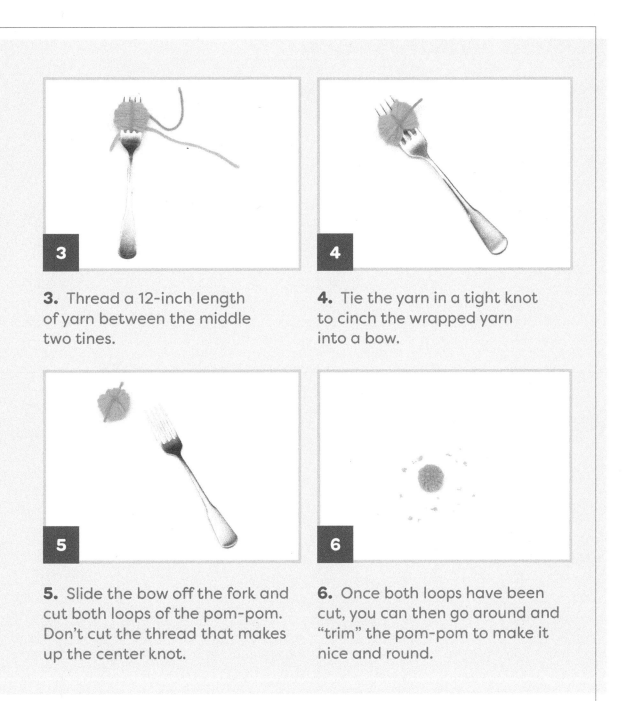

3. Thread a 12-inch length of yarn between the middle two tines.

4. Tie the yarn in a tight knot to cinch the wrapped yarn into a bow.

5. Slide the bow off the fork and cut both loops of the pom-pom. Don't cut the thread that makes up the center knot.

6. Once both loops have been cut, you can then go around and "trim" the pom-pom to make it nice and round.

Felted Wool Acorns ◆❗

Would a squirrel be fooled by a felted wool acorn? Before wool gets made into yarn or your favorite sweater, it can be purchased raw as roving. This roving can be "agitated," or rolled, into fun colorful balls that you can then use to fill a trinket dish, string like a bead, or (for some extra fun) top with an acorn cap.

MESSY METER

1   2   3   4   〈5〉

WHAT YOU NEED:

- Raw, 100 percent wool roving
- Warm soapy water
- Hot glue gun
- Glue sticks
- Acorn caps
- Needle (optional)
- Embroidery floss (optional)

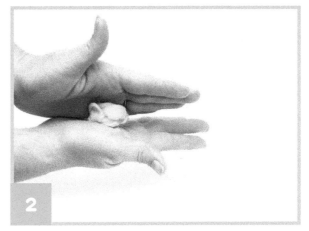

1. Roving will come in loose strands. Tear off approximately 6 inches for a small bead. Submerge the roving into the warm soapy water.

2. Squeeze out excess water and begin rolling the roving in your hand like you would a piece of clay to form a ball shape. This is called agitating the wool.

Continued →

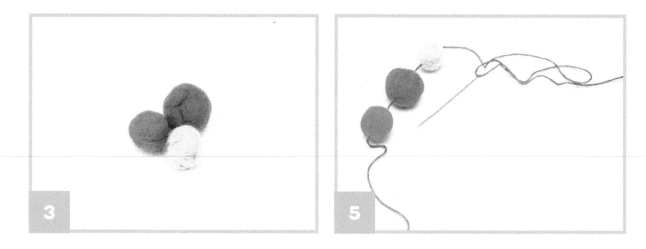

3. Repeat dipping into warm water and rolling the wool between your palms until a tight ball forms. This takes about 3 to 4 dips in the water and 10 minutes of agitating.

4. Ask an adult to help you hot glue small acorn caps on top of the balls.

5. As an alternative, you can also string the felt balls together as a necklace. Thread a needle with embroidery floss and push the needle through each felt ball. Tie the ends closed and you have a brand-new necklace.

Sun Printing

With a little patience, paint, and sunlight, you can use the sun to "develop" an image on fabric. It's like nature's camera. Once you learn this technique, you'll want to try sun printing on everything.

MESSY METER

1 2 3 4 5

WHAT YOU NEED:

- Acrylic craft paint
- Water
- Bowl
- Large paintbrush
- Cotton fabric
- Leaves

Continued →

Sun Printing, continued

1. Mix water and craft paint in a one-to-one ratio in a bowl. Lay the fabric on a flat surface outside in a sunny spot. Use a large paintbrush to cover the fabric with the mixture.

2. While the fabric is still wet, place a variety of leaves face-down on the surface. Press them down so that the edges make good contact.

3. Leave the fabric in the sun for 2 to 3 hours. When the fabric has dried, remove and discard the leaves.

4. Have fun experimenting with different colors of paint, different types of leaves, and other combinations!

Seed Balls

Have you ever walked past an empty patch of soil and thought to yourself, "Wow, this spot could really use some wildflowers!"? Now you can make that happen. Seed balls can be tossed to spread a little floral joy in all kinds of places, including your own backyard! Remember to make sure the seeds you use are native to the area and that you always ask permission before dropping a ball in someone's yard. Happy seed spreading!

MESSY METER

1 2 3 4 5

WHAT YOU NEED:

- Natural air-dry clay
- Wildflower seeds
- Planting soil
- Dried flowers
- Water

Continued →

Seed Balls, continued

1. Soak seeds in water for 12 hours. This will help ensure your seed balls actually work.

2. Pinch off pieces of air-dry clay the size of small bouncy balls. Press each one into the shape of a small bowl.

3. Fill each of the clay bowls with a little bit of planting soil.

4. Sprinkle 10 to 20 of the wildflower seeds atop each bowl of dirt.

5

5. Close the bowl by pinching together two sides to form a taco. Next fold the other two sides in towards the center. Roll this into a ball using the palms of your hands.

6. Roll your seed balls into a bit of planting soil and dried flowers for some color. Allow the balls to dry completely, and when you find the perfect spot that needs a bit of color, toss the seed ball.

Pressed Leaf Lanterns ◆

Make your own nature-inspired nightlight in no time. Go for a scavenging hike and gather a few small leaves or flowers that catch your eye; they will be the decorative centerpiece to your lantern.

MESSY METER

1   2   3   4   5

WHAT YOU NEED:

- Small leaves
- Wax paper
- 16 wooden craft sticks
- Dish towel
- Iron
- Scissors
- Hot glue gun
- Glue sticks
- Pom-poms (optional)
- Battery-operated tea light

1. Choose colorful leaves for your lantern and set them aside. Lay out 4 craft sticks in a square to give you a rough idea of how large your sheets of wax paper should be. Cut a sheet that is double that size and fold it in half. Arrange the leaves inside the folded wax paper.

2. Cover the wax paper with a dish towel or cloth and iron it on medium heat. Move the iron over the covered wax paper for 20 seconds and check to see if the pieces of wax paper have fused together. If not, continue ironing for another 20 seconds. Set the fused wax paper aside. Repeat steps 1 and 2 three more times to create 4 sheets of leaves fused in wax paper.

Continued →

3. Take 4 craft sticks and glue them into a square. Repeat 3 more times so that you have 4 squares total. These will act as the frame for your lantern.

4. Glue a sheet of fused wax paper to each of the craft stick frames. Use scissors to trim off excess paper around the edges.

5. Ask for an adult's help to assemble and attach all 4 pieces of the lantern walls together using hot glue.

6. Feel free to cover the edges with ball fringe or pom-poms.

7. Place a small battery-operated light inside and watch your new lantern glow. If you are making this in the summer and there are no colorful leaves to be found, try using pressed flowers instead.

Rolled Magazine Storage

This adorable project scores double recycling points. Not only are you giving an old cardboard box a new use, the colorful makeover is provided by old magazines. Once you learn to roll the tube shape, the rest is just a matter of gluing. No empty box around your house will ever stay plain and boring again.

MESSY METER

WHAT YOU NEED:

- Old magazines
- Pencil or paintbrush
- Glue stick
- Craft glue
- Cardboard box with top flaps removed (shoebox size works great)
- Scissors

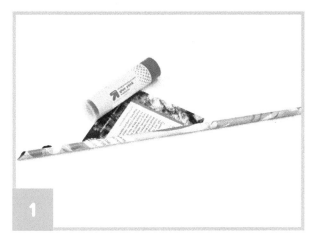

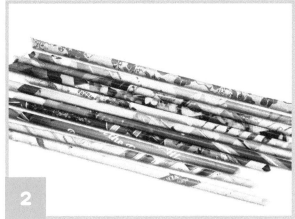

1. Cut out colorful pages from old magazines and roll each page up into tight straw shapes. Roll from one corner to the opposite corner. Use a pencil or the end of a paintbrush if that helps to form the straw shapes. When you're nearly done rolling a page, apply the glue stick to the last triangle to fasten.

2. Continue making magazine paper straws until you have enough to cover the outer edge of the cardboard box.

Continued →

3. Apply craft glue to one small section at a time of the cardboard box. While the glue is still wet, add the magazine straws.

4. Repeat step 3 until the entire box is covered.

5. Allow the glue to dry completely. Trim the magazine rolls to be even with the top of the box. Once dry and trimmed, fill the box with toys, trinkets, or craft supplies.

Recycled Hanging Bottle Planter ◆!

Ever notice how the bottoms of certain plastic bottles look a lot like animal paws? Yeah, me too. Reuse that plastic bottle and turn it into an adorable hanging basket for plants—and a new furry friend.

MESSY METER

◆1 ◆2 ◆3 ◆4 ◇5

WHAT YOU NEED:

- Clean, empty plastic bottle with labels removed
- Permanent marker
- Multi-surface craft paint
- Paintbrush
- Hole punch
- Leather cording
- Small plant
- Decoupage medium

Continued →

Recycled Hanging Bottle Planter, continued

WHAT YOU DO:

1. Use a permanent marker to draw on your design.

2. Ask an adult for help cutting out your design. This will remove the top of the bottle.

3. Paint the outside of the bottle. You may need to apply 2 to 3 coats, allowing to dry between coats.

4. Once it's dry, add features like a nose, eyes, and more. Give your planter some character!

5. Using a hole punch, make 4 holes in the top of the planter. Each hole should be approximately ½ inch from the rim, and the holes should be spaced equally apart.

6. Cut a piece of 15-inch leather cording. Tie a knot larger than the hole you just punched in one end of the cording. Lace through the first hole.

Continued →

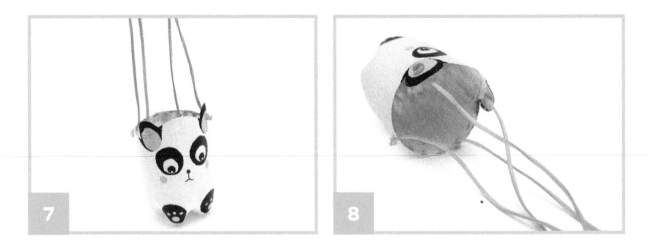

7. Put the other end of the cording in the hole diagonal from it. Tie another knot on the outside of the planter larger than the hole. Trim off any excess.

8. Repeat this same process with the remaining two holes and a second piece of cording. When you have completed it the cording should make an X.

9. Add your favorite type of plant to the bottle. For hanging planters, you want plants that grow vines, such as an ivy plant.

Too Cute Trinket Jars

Trinket jars have endless storage uses, and the best part is they are recycled from old jars and toys. You can make them any size you want. As long as the lid screws on, the container is a contender. We are going to be using mason jars, but baby food containers, vitamin bottles, and pasta sauce jars all work great, too.

MESSY METER

1 2 3 4 ‹5›

WHAT YOU NEED:

- Empty jars
- Small plastic toys
- Glue
- Multi-surface craft paint
- Paintbrush
- Decorative trim
- Pom-poms

Continued →

Too Cute Trinket Jars, continued

1. Remove the lids. Glue one small plastic toy onto each lid. Let glue dry.

2. Apply craft paint to lids and toys. Apply 2 to 3 coats, allowing paint to dry completely between coats.

3. Embellish toys and lids with decorative trim and pom-poms using craft glue.

4. Store anything in the jars—office supplies, craft supplies, or knickknacks—and keep your closets organized.

Custom String Lights ◆

If you thought cardboard-tube crafts were for preschoolers, you thought wrong. These spent tubes get an upgrade with the help of decorative napkins, making custom string lights that will be the envy of all your friends.

MESSY METER

1 2 3 4 5

WHAT YOU NEED:

- Empty paper towel rolls
- Ruler
- Pencil
- Scissors
- Hole punch
- Decorative napkins
- Ready-made string lights
- Decoupage medium
- Paint
- Glue
- Pom-poms

Continued →

Custom String Lights, continued

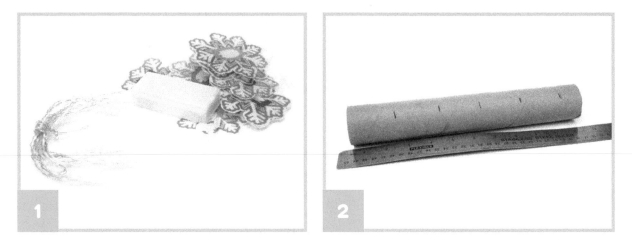

1. If your string lights came with decorative covers, remove and save them for another project.

2. Use a ruler and mark a spot every 2 inches along your cardboard tube.

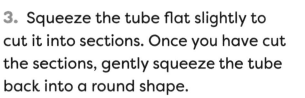

3. Squeeze the tube flat slightly to cut it into sections. Once you have cut the sections, gently squeeze the tube back into a round shape.

4. Cut as many 2-inch sections of paper towel tube as you have lights on the strand.

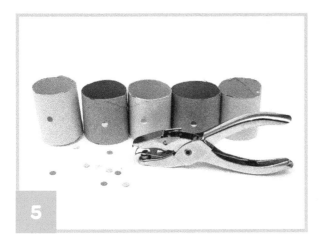

5. Use a hole punch to make a hole in the center of each tube. This will be where your light goes into the tube.

6. Find something like a small lid with a slightly larger circumference than the paper towel tube. Trace this lid onto a decorative napkin using a pen or pencil. Cut out the circle with scissors. Remember that your tubes have two ends, so if your strand has 9 lights, you will need 18 circles of napkin.

Continued →

Custom String Lights, continued

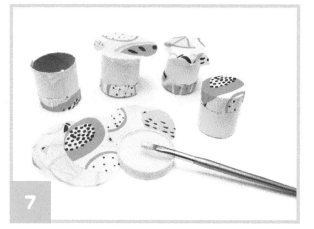

7. Paint the tubes a festive color or leave them plain. Once the paint has dried, use a decoupage medium to apply one circle of napkin to each end of the cardboard tube. Start by covering the entire edge in decoupage, place napkin on top, fold down to touch in a few spots, and use a paintbrush and more decoupage medium to adhere completely. Repeat on both ends of all of the cardboard tubes.

8. Cover the extra napkin with paint. If you want to accent with polka dots or your favorite colorful pattern, go for it.

9. Insert the light into the hole you punched. Ask an adult for help to add a dab of hot glue to hold each light in place. Feel free to also add pom-poms.

10. Plug your lights in, hang, and enjoy! The perfect ambient light, and with so many different napkins out there, you could make a new set for every day of the week.

GLOSSARY

Charm tag: A jewelry finding that has a small surface to glue something onto and a loop on the top for hanging it on a cord or chain.

Decoupage medium: A thick, glue-like liquid traditionally used to decorate objects with paper or used as a protective top coat.

Laundry cording: Typically found in the hardware department, this cotton cording is used to hang laundry out to dry.

Multi-surface craft paint: This paint will say on the bottle that it can be used on various surfaces, such as plastic.

Ombré: A pattern of colors that blend or shade into each other, particularly in which the colors are graduated from light to dark.

Rug canvas: Plastic grid-like material used for latch hooking.

Sizing: A chemical that has been added to most new clothing, especially T-shirts, to prevent them from being marked or stained at the store.

Split ring: Often seen on a keychain, a split ring is actually two connected rings with a slight split, and keys and other things can be threaded onto it.

Sponge dauber: Paintbrushes with sponge tips in various round sizes used for making polka dots.

Stiffened craft felt: These are sheets of craft felt that have been slightly stiffened through a treatment process.

RESOURCES

- Amazon
- Hobby Lobby
- Kim Geiser – Coloring Book Pages for Shrink Plastic Flair amazon.com/Kim-Geiser /e/B01N060OKZ
- Michaels

- Plaid Crafts – Stencils used for sashiko patches and watercolor resist plaidonline.com
- Target
- Walmart

INDEX

B

Bath bombs, 90–93
Best Friend Doughnut Charm
    Necklaces, 86–89
Bubbles, 36–38

C

Cardboard, xi
Cards, 83–85
Cereal-Box Puppet Theater, 27
Chalk, 34–35
Charm tags, 86–89, 162
Cookie Cutter Ring Dishes, 111–113
Craft glue, xi
Craft paint, x
Custom String Lights, 157–161

D

Decoupage medium, xi, 162
DIY Pom-Poms, 128–129
Drip Pots, 96–98

E

Easy Woven Wall Hanging, 106–108
Embroidery Hoop Wall
    Pocket, 103–105

F

Faux Sashiko Denim Patches,
    54–55
Felted Wool Acorns, 136–138
Fluffy and Fun Chalkboard
    Slime, 31–33
Foil art, 20–21

G

Giant-Bubble Solution, 38
Giant Bubble Wand, 36–38
Glow-in-the-Dark Chalk, 34–35
Glues, x–xi
Groovy Gravel Trays, 124–125

H

Hot glue gun, x–xi

I

Ice dyeing, 46–48
Irresistible Watercolor Resist
    Art, 7–8

J

Jewelry, 52–53, 86–89

K

Key chains, 68–70

L

Lanterns, 144–147
Laundry cording, 118–120, 162

M

Marbling, 4–6
Materials, x–xi
Melty Bead Picture Frame, 114–117
Mindful Jars, 39–40
Mini Pom-Poms, 134–135
Modern Art on Wood, 2–3
Multi-surface craft paint, 162

N

No-Kill Cardboard Cactus, 9–11
No-Sew Felt Enamel Pin
    Banner, 109–110
No-Sew Felt Pillow, 99–102
No-Sew Scrunchies, 49–51

O

Ombré, 162

P

Paintbrushes, x
Painted Rock People, 41–43
Painting, 18–19, 41–43.
    See also Watercolor
Pantyhose Silk Screen, 56–59
Paper Bag Hanging Stars, 121–123
Paper Clip and Washi Tape
    Jewelry, 52–53
Patches, 54–55
Petite Pom-Pom Rug, 126–127
Picture frames, 114–117
Pillows, 99–102
Planters, 151–154
Pom-poms, 126–129, 134–135
Pressed Leaf Lanterns, 144–147
Printing, 16–17, 139–140

R

Rainbow Bath Bombs, 90–93
Recycled Hanging Bottle
    Planter, 151–154
Recycled Wrapped Vase, 132–133
Repeat patterns, 16–17
Rolled Magazine Storage, 148–150

Rolling-Pin Printing, 16–17
Rooty Tooty Fruity Foil Art, 20–21
Rug canvas, 126–127, 162

S

Safety, xi
Sashiko, 54–55
Scrunchies, 49–51
Seed Balls, 141–143
Shaving Cream Marbling, 4–6
Shrink Plastic Flair, 65–67
Silk screening, 56–59
Sizing, 162
Slime, 31–33
Soap Pops, 76–78
Split rings, 68–70, 162
Sponge daubers, 118–120, 162
Spoon Puppets, 24–26

Sticker Resist T-Shirt, 71–73
Stiffened craft felt, 109–110, 162
Stitched Greeting Cards, 83–85
String lights, 157–161
Sunglass case, 60–62
Sun Printing, 139–140
Super Cool Ice Dyeing, 46–48
Supplies, x–xi

T

Taco Sunglass Case, 60–62
Tassel Key Chains, 68–70
Tie-Dye Shoes, 63–64
Tin Can Robots, 28–30
Tips and tricks, xii–xiii
Too Cute Trinket Jars, 155–156
Tools, x–xi
T-Shirt Notebook, 79–82

V

Vases, 132–133

W

Washi tape, 52–53
Watercolor, 7–8
Way Out Weaving, 12–15
Weaving, 12–15, 106–108
Wrapped Desk Caddy,
    118–120

Y

Yarn, x
Yarn Painting, 18–19

ACKNOWLEDGMENTS

Thank you to my editors, Jeanine Le Ny and Eliza Kirby, for all your hand-holding; Jennifer M. Ramos for the fabulous pictures; and Kim Geiser and Plaid Crafts for letting me use your rad art!

ABOUT THE AUTHOR

Jennifer Perkins is a mother of two crafty and adorable kidlets living in Austin, TX. Jennifer had them finger painting with chocolate pudding as babies, and they still love getting artsy with their mom to this day. (Side note: They now use paint instead of pudding.) Jennifer's own mother was ridiculously crafty, always jumping from one medium and passion to another. This influence started Jennifer down her own path as a maker. One of her earliest DIY memories is making and selling earrings out of fishing lures at a family garage sale—and the rest is history! Her tag line is "Crafts, kitsch, and kids," but color and maybe Christmas trees should also be added to that list. Her crafty handiwork has been featured in places like *Country Living*, *Better Homes and Gardens*, HGTV, and more. When she is not gluing pom-poms on things, she can be found roaming the aisles of a thrift store, walking her dogs (while in paint-covered pants) alongside her equally creative husband, or planning over-the-top decorations for whatever the next major (or minor) holiday is on the horizon.

jenniferperkins.com
Instagram @jenniferperkins
Facebook @iamjenperkins